Max Sørensen

Professor, dr. jur.

Max Sørensen

En Bibliografi
A Bibliography

AARHUS UNIVERSITY PRESS

AARHUS UNIVERSITY PRESS
Aarhus University
DK-8000 Aarhus C

Indhold

Contents

Forord

Da min afdøde mand professor dr. jur. Max Sørensens videnskabelige produktion er offentliggjort i forskellige lande og på forskellige sprog håber jeg med denne bibliografi at kunne imødekomme ønsker om en samlet oversigt over hans forfatterskab. Samtidig har det været mig en glæde på denne måde at kunne bidrage til at bevare mindet om min mand.

Det er mit håb at bibliografien bedre end mange ord vil give indtryk af min mands velkendte flid og vidtspændende kundskaber på de mange områder af den juridiske videnskab, han beskæftigede sig med.

I erindring om min mands livslange arbejde for problemerne om menneskerettighederne har jeg fundet det naturligt at indlede bibliografien med et enkelt eksempel fra dette område, nemlig min mands rapport til det 4. internationale Kolloqvium om den Europæiske Menneskerettigheds Konvention, afholdt i Rom fra 5. til 8. november 1975, offentliggjort på engelsk af The Council of Europe, Strasbourg i 1975 (H/Coll. (75) 2-Or. fr.) under titlen: »Do the rights set forth in The European Convention on Human Rights in 1950 have the same significance in 1975?«

Jeg takker min mands kollega og ven, professor, dr.jur. Carl Aage Nørgaard for hans tilladelse til som indledning til bibliografien at bringe den nekrolog over min mand, som han skrev til Aarskrift for Aarhus Universitet for 1981, samt for hans version af nekrologen på engelsk, ligesom jeg takker ham for hjælp og støtte under udarbejdelsen af bibliografien.

En ganske særlig tak retter jeg til forskningsbibliotekar ved Det kongelige Bibliotek, cand.jur. Jens Søndergaard, som med kyndighed og omhu har gennemset, rettet og suppleret mit manuskript og udarbejdet den summariske systematiske del B af bibliografien.

Endelig takker jeg bibliotekar ved Aarhus Universitets juridiske bibliotek, cand.jur. Karl Georg Schmidt for megen hjælpsomhed under udarbejdelsen af bibliografien.

Risskov, august 1988   *Ellen Max Sørensen*

Preface

My late husband, professor doctor juris Max Sørensen's books and articles have been published in various countries and in various languages. It is my intention and hope that the present bibliography may comply with wishes for a complete survey of his works. In addition, it has been a pleasure for me in this way to contribute to preserve the memory of my husband.

It is also my hope that the bibliography, better than many words, will bear witness of my husband's well known diligence and comprehensive knowledge within the various fields of the science of law to which he devoted himself.

Throughout his career, the work for the protection of Human Rights occupied my husband. I have therefore found it appropriate to include in the bibliography an example from this field, namely his report to the Fourth International Colloquy about the European Convention on Human Rights, which took place in Rome from 5-8 November 1975. (H/Coll. (75) 2-Or. fr.) under the title: "Do the rights set forth in The European Convention on Human Rights in 1950 have the same significance in 1975?"

I express my thanks to my husband's collegue and friend, professor, doctor juris Carl Aage Nørgaard, for his permission to include in the bibliography his obituary about my husband, which appeared in the Yearbook of Aarhus University for 1981, and for his help and encouragement during my work with the bibliography.

I offer sincere thanks to the Law Librarian at the Royal Library in Copenhagen, candidatus juris Jens Søndergaard, who with great care and knowledge has revised and supplemented my manuscript and elaborated the summary systematic part B of the bibliography.

Finally I thank the librarian at the Law Library at Aarhus University, candidatus juris Karl Georg Schmidt, for his kind assistance during my work with the bibliography.

Risskov, August 1988   *Ellen Max Sørensen*

Max Sørensen

19. februar 1913 - 11. oktober 1981

Max Sørensen kom til Aarhus Universitet i 1947, da han som 34-årig blev udnævnt til professor i retsvidenskab med arbejdsfelt inden for den offentlige rets område.

Allerede i sin studietid nærede Max Sørensen en levende interesse for folkeretten og gav bevis for sine videnskabelige evner, da han i 1934 besvarede Københavns Universitets prisopgave, om betingelserne for traktaters afslutning, og modtog guldmedalje for besvarelsen. Efter sin embedseksamen i 1938 blev Max Sørensen ansat i udenrigsministeriet, hvor han gjorde tjeneste dels herhjemme og dels i Bern og London indtil 1947. Sideløbende med arbejdet i udenrigsministeriet fortsatte han sit videnskabelige arbejde og erhvervede i 1946 den juridiske doktorgrad for afhandlingen »Les Sources du Droit International«.

Ved sin tiltrædelse af professoratet ved Aarhus Universitet i 1947 påtog Max Sørensen sig en omfattende undervisningsbyrde, idet han varetog undervisning og eksamen i de tre fag statsforfatningsret, forvaltningsret og folkeret. I de følgende år skete der under hans ledelse først en langsom, senere – med det hastigt stigende studentertal – en hurtigere udvidelse af lærerstaben på området.

Da han i 1972 efter 25 års gerning ved Aarhus Universitet trak sig tilbage for at tiltræde stillingen som dommer i EF's domstol, var der beskæftiget 12 heltidsansatte lærere ved Institut for offentlig ret, som han havde taget initiativet til at oprette i 1960.

Max Sørensens undervisning vil utvivlsomt af alle, der har deltaget i den, blive husket som højdepunkter i det juridiske studium. Han var altid uhyre velforberedt og var i stand til at foretage tilbundsgående analyser af svært tilgængelige problemer på en sådan måde, at metoden og tankegangen blev klar for enhver student, som arbejdede med stoffet. Samtidig placerede han enkeltproblemerne i den sammenhæng, hvor de hørte hjemme, således at overblikket

11

bevaredes. Det er utvivlsomt, at Max Sørensen gennem sin undervisning har præget sine studenter i usædvanlig grad. Hans forelæsninger var båret af tankens og sprogets klarhed, et ufravigeligt krav om saglighed og objektivitet, isprængt stilfærdig humor. Bag den ydre form fornemmede de studerende en, omend sjældent direkte formuleret, trang til at delagtiggøre dem i de høje menneskelige idealer han troede på.

Ved siden af sine øvrige opgaver tog Max Sørensen engageret del i det administrative arbejde, såvel på konsistorie- som fakultetsniveau. Han var leder af Institut for offentlig ret i de første opbygningsår og var den altid inspirerende igangsætter og vejleder for de videnskabelige medarbejdere ved instituttet.

Fra første færd optog spørgsmålet om samfundsvidenskabernes udvikling og betydning Max Sørensen levende og på baggrund af sin internationale erfaring anså han det som en mangel, at Political Science eller Statskundskab ikke eksisterede som en selvstændig akademisk disciplin her i landet. Allerede i 1949 fremsatte han et konkret forslag om et statskundskabsstudium. I de følgende år arbejdede han stærkt støttet af professor dr. phil. Troels Fink videre med disse tanker, som realiseredes ved oprettelsen af statskundskabsstudiet ved Aarhus Universitet i 1958. I de første år varetog Max Sørensen undervisningen i faget International Organisation ved det nye studium og omfattede resten af sit liv dette studium med varm interesse.

Max Sørensen markerede sig tidligt som en selvstændig og original forsker og blev snart anerkendt som en af de mest fremragende inden for retsvidenskaben. I disputatsen »Les Sources du Droit International«, der i dag overalt anses som en klassiker i den folkeretlige litteratur, foretages en indgående analyse af retspraksis fra den mellemfolkelige domstol i Haag, som var oprettet i 1920. Problemet om folkerettens kilder hørte til de mest omdebatterede i den folkeretlige teori og problemet opfattedes traditionelt som normativt – man undersøgte med andre ord, hvilke synspunkter dommeren bør lægge til grund for sin afgørelse. Det afgørende nye var, at Max Sørensen konsekvent anvendte en analytisk-deskriptiv metode og lagde vægt på de faktorer, som domstolen faktisk fulgte i sin praksis.

I 1960 holdt Max Sørensen hovedforelæsningsrækken ved Academie de Droit International i Haag. Forelæsningerne, der er udgivet under titlen »Principes de Droit International Public« behandler alle folkerettens hovedproblemer og er i dag en højt værdsat grundlæggende fremstilling inden for den internationale ret. I begyndelsen af 1960erne tog Carnegie Endowment for International Peace initiativet til udgivelsen af en stor moderne fremstilling af folkeretten. Max Sørensen blev udpeget som hovedredaktør og 12 fremtrædende folkeretsspecialister påtog sig at skrive de enkelte afsnit. Resultatet forelå i 1968 som »Manual of Public International Law« – et værk på næsten 1000 sider. Max Sørensen skrev kapitlet »Institutionalized International Co-operation in Economic, Social and Cultural Fields« og ydede desuden en enestående indsats med at tilrettelægge og koordinere det samlede arbejde, således at værket trods forfatternes forskelligheder fremtræder som en helhed, der i dag som lære- og håndbog er standardlæsning for enhver, der dyrker folkeretten.

Det vil føre for vidt på dette sted at omtale rækken af Max Sørensens bøger og mangfoldige afhandlinger om folkeretlige emner. Som en særlig gruppe af arbejder bør dog nævnes hans mange afhandlinger om den internationale beskyttelse af menneskerettigheder. På dette område var Max Sørensen anerkendt som en af vor tids største eksperter både på grund af sit praktiske arbejde og på grund af sine dybtgående analyser af vanskelige fortolkningsspørgsmål.

Selv om Max Sørensens videnskabelige hovedindsats har ligget på den internationale rets område, har han tillige skrevet vægtige afhandlinger om centrale problemer i dansk statsforfatningsret og forvaltningsret – i første række lærebogen »Statsforfatningsret« fra 1969. Det var naturligt, at han med sin faste tro på værdien og nødvendigheden af internationalt samarbejde særligt interesserede sig for en udvikling af dansk forfatningsret, som kunne udbygge mulighederne for dansk deltagelse i et sådant samarbejde. Han havde da også en væsentlig indflydelse på udformningen af bestemmelsen om suverænitetsafgivelse i § 20 i grundloven af 1953, som muliggjorde Danmarks tilslutning til internationale fællesskaber.

Den indsats, Max Sørensen har ydet som forsker og universitetslærer er af en sådan standard og et sådant omfang, at den i sig selv måtte synes vanskelig at overkomme. Sideløbende hermed påtog han sig imidlertid en række betydningsfulde offentlige opgaver; i årene fra 1956 til 1972 varetog han det tidskrævende hverv som udenrigsministeriets rådgiver i folkeret. Desuden deltog han i disse år som dansk repræsentant i en række internationale organer og konferencer, hvor han satte sit præg på talrige betydningsfulde afgørelser. Det var f.eks. tilfældet på FN's havretskonferencer i 1958 og 1960, hvor han var chef for den danske delegation.

Dommergerningen ved en international domstol oplevede Max Sørensen første gang 1968-69, da han var udpeget som dommer ad hoc i den internationale domstol i Haag ved behandlingen af sagen om sokkelgrænsen i Nordsøen. Ved Danmarks tilslutning til EF var det naturligt, at Max Sørensen blev opfordret til og påtog sig det byrdefulde hverv som den første danske dommer i EF-domstolen i Luxembourg for perioden indtil 1979.

Blandt de mange internationale opgaver Max Sørensen beskæftigede sig med var vel arbejdet for beskyttelse af menneskerettigheder, som optog ham livet igennem, det han anså for mest betydningsfuldt inden for den internationale retsorden. Allerede i 1949 blev han udpeget til medlem af FN's kommission for menneskerettigheder og var 1954-56 formand for underkommissionen for beskyttelse af mindretal. I 18 år fra 1955 var han dansk medlem af den europæiske menneskerettighedskommission i Strasbourg, heraf 5 år som kommissionens præsident og endelig var han fra 1980 til 1981 dommer i den europæiske menneskerettighedsdomstol. Hans arbejde på dette område var på een gang præget af hans fundamentale tro på nødvendigheden af en international beskyttelse af det enkelte menneske over for statsmagten og en klar forståelse af, at udviklingen måtte ske inden for rammerne af de bestående internationale overenskomster. Gennem sit arbejde i menneskerettighedsorganisationerne har Max Sørensen øvet en indflydelse, som ikke overgås af nogen anden samtidig og hans indsats på dette område har sat sig blivende og markante spor.

Det er vanskeligt at fremhæve på hvilket område af det vidt spændende arbejdsfelt han beskæftigede sig med, Max Sørensen har ydet den mest skelsættende indsats. Alt hvad han beskæftigede sig med blev behandlet med grundighed og en næsten overmenneskelig flid og resultaterne af hans arbejde var altid af ubestridig kvalitet.

Trods den anerkendelse og beundring Max Sørensen var genstand for, bevarede han sin dybe og ægte beskedenhed og accepterede kun sjældent de æresbevisninger, som blev ham tilbudt. Han glædede sig dog over udnævnelsen til æresdoktor ved universitetet i

14

Kiel i 1964 og ikke mindst over den meddelelse, han modtog kort før sin død om udnævnelse til æresdoktor ved universitetet i Strasbourg, som han var nært knyttet til. Herhjemme modtog Max Sørensen Fortjenstmedaljen i guld, efter han var fratrådt som dommer i Luxembourg.

Den indsats, som Max Sørensen ydede, var sikkert kun mulig, fordi han havde evnen til at hente inspiration og nye kræfter fra mange kilder, ikke mindst gennem sin dybe og ægte glæde for naturen og alt levende. Det der imidlertid gennem alle årene betød mere end noget andet for ham, var ægteskabet med Ellen Max Sørensen. Det aldrig svigtende grundlag for ham og hans indsats var deres fine, fortrolige fællesskab.

Max Sørensen nød respekt og anerkendelse herhjemme og i udlandet, som kun sjældent bliver en dansk jurist til del. De, som har kendt ham, studenter og medarbejdere vil bevare erindringen om ham, ikke blot som den fremragende jurist, men tillige som et hjertevarmt menneske med høje idealer og en ukuelig tro på, at disse idealer kan virkeliggøres gennem en utrættelig arbejdsindsats. Max Sørensen gav gennem sit eget liv og virke det bedste eksempel.

Carl Aage Nørgaard

Max Sørensen

February 19, 1913 - October 11, 1981

Max Sørensen was appointed professor in jurisprudence at the University of Aarhus in 1947, at only 34 years of age.

From the very beginning of his law study, international law fascinated Max Sørensen and in 1934 as a student at the University in Copenhagen he received the highest prize for young scholars, the University's gold medal, as a reward for a dissertation on the subject of Conclusion of International Treaties.

Having graduated as a lawyer in 1938, Max Sørensen commenced his career in the Danish Ministry for Foreign Affairs, where during the following years he performed his duties in Copenhagen, Berne and London until 1947. During his years in the foreign service, he continued his research in International Public Law and wrote the thesis "Les Sources du Droit International", for which the degree of Doctor Juris was conferred on him.

During the first years as a professor at the University of Aarhus, Max Sørensen assumed an extensive burden of work carrying out teaching and examination, not only in Public International Law but also at the same time in Danish Constitutional Law and Administrative Law. Under his leadership, however, the teaching and research staff gradually increased in the following years.

In 1960 Max Sørensen took the initiative to establish the Institute of Public Law, which counted a permanent staff of 12 lawyers when, in 1972, he retired from the University to take up his chair as the first Danish judge to the European Court of Justice in Luxembourg.

Undoubtedly Max Sørensen's students will remember his lectures as the high points of their law studies. Always thoroughly prepared, he was able to undertake profound analyses of difficult problems in such a way that the method and line of thought were understood by every student engaged in the problems. At the same time he had the ability to place the details in their right context and maintain the overall point of view. His lectures were hallmarked by clarity of thinking and expression, rigorous observance of the requirements of impartiality and objectivity, and at the same time, a touch of gentle humour. The outstanding quality of the lectures made a strong and lasting impression on his students and although he seldom expressed it directly his students were always aware of his desire to convey the moral horizons and the high human ideals in which he himself believed.

Besides his teaching and research, Max Sørensen took an active part in the administrative work of the University at all levels. He was the head of the Institute of Public Law in the first difficult years, and he was always the inspiring initiator and guide for the research staff of the Institute.

Throughout his university career, Max Sørensen took a vivid interest in the particular problems regarding the importance and development of the social sciences, and based on his international experience he considered it a disadvantage that political science did not exist as an independent academic study in Denmark. In 1949 he made the first concrete proposal for teaching and research in political science at the University of Aarhus. During the following years he continued to work on these ideas and projects, supported by professor, dr.phil. Troels Fink, and in 1958 the ideas materialized with the creation of the Faculty of Political Science at the University of Aarhus. For some years Max Sørensen lectured on the subject of International Organization at the new faculty to which he was devoted for the rest of his life.

Max Sørensen was an independent and original scholar and was early recognized as one of the most outstanding within the field of jurisprudence. In his thesis "Les Sources du Droit International", today considered a milestone in the doctrine of International Law, he undertook a profound analysis of the case law from the Permanent Court of International Justice in the Hague. The sources of international law was one of the most controversial problems in the doctrine of international law and was traditionally dealt with as a normative problem, in other words it was discussed on which grounds a judge ought to base his decisions. The fundamental change was that Max Sørensen consistently used an analytic-descriptive method and investigated on which reasons the Court in fact based its judgements.

In 1960 Max Sørensen delivered the principal course of lectures in public international law at the Académie de Droit International at the Hague. The lectures, published under the title "Principes de Droit International Public", deal with all the main problems of public international law and are today highly esteemed as a fundamental work in this field.

In the early 1960s the Carnegie Endowment for International Peace took the initiative to publish a large modern textbook on international law. Max Sørensen was appointed editor-in-chief and twelve specialists in public international law were charged with the task of writing the different chapters. The result of their work was published in 1968 under the title "Manual of Public International Law" – a book of about 1000 pages. Besides writing the chapter "Institutionalized International Co-operation in Economic, Social and Cultural Fields", Max Sørensen planned and coordinated the work in an eminent way with the result that the book, in spite of its different authors, forms a whole and is today an indispensable standard textbook for everybody working within the field of public international law.

Max Sørensen has written numerous books and papers on international law subjects. One group, however, deserves special mentioning, namely his many books and articles regarding the international protection of human rights. In this field, Max Sørensen was recognized as one of the greatest experts of our time, both as a practitioner and a scholar.

Although Max Sørensen's main scientific contribution has been within the field of international law he has at the same time written important books and articles on central problems of Danish Constitutional Law and Administrative law, above all the textbook "Statsforfatningsret" ("Constitutional Law") from 1969. With his profound belief in the necessity and value of international cooperation it was natural that he took special interest in a development of Danish Constitutional Law that could facilitate Denmark's possibilities for participation in international cooperation. In this respect he played an important role in the drafting of a new clause regarding transfer of sovereignty in the Danish constitution of 1953 which made it possible for Denmark to join supra-national organizations.

Max Sørensen's achievements as a teacher and a scholar are of such high standard and proportions that it is difficult to comprehend how it was possible for him to overcome the work. Nevertheless, in addition to his professorship he assumed a number of important public functions such as the time-consuming office of legal adviser to the Ministry of Foreign Affairs from 1956 to 1972. Moreover, during this period he also participated as Danish representative in a number of international organs and conferences where he had influence on numerous important decisions. This was, for instance, the case at the United Nations' conferences on the Law of the Sea in 1958 and 1960 where he was the leader of the Danish delegation.

In 1968 Max Sørensen was appointed judge ad hoc to the International Court at the Hauge in the case concerning the continental shelf in the North Sea. When Denmark joined the European Communities, it was a matter of course that Max Sørensen was appointed to the important and difficult office as the first Danish judge on the European Court of Justice in Luxembourg for the period until 1979.

Among the many different aspects of international organization and cooperation in which Max Sørensen was involved he considered the international protection of human rights as the most fundamental within the entire international legal order. In 1949 he became a member of the United Nations' Commission for Human Rights and from 1954-56 he served as president of the Sub-commission for Protection of Minorities. During 18 years, from 1955 until 1973, he was a member of the Eureopean Commission of Human Rights, serving 5 years as president of the Commission. Finally, from 1980 and until his death in 1981 he was a judge on the European Court of Human Rights. His work in this field was always influenced by his fundamental belief in the need for international protection of the individual against the state, combined with the realistic understanding that this can only be achieved through peaceful development within the framework of international organization. No one of our generation has influenced the work for the protection of human rights more than Max Sørensen, and his efforts in this field have been of lasting and marked importance.

In spite of all the recognition and admiration he received Max

Sørensen always preserved his profound and genuine modesty and seldom accepted the honours which he was offered. It was, however, a pleasure for him to receive the degree of Doctor Honoris Causa at the University in Kiel in 1964, and he was happy when he shortly before his death was informed of his nomination as Doctor Honoris Causa at the University of Strasbourg with which he had close connections. In Denmark the Queen awarded him one of the highest Danish honours, Fortjenstmedaljen i Guld (the Order of Merit in gold) after his retirement as a judge in Luxembourg.

Max Sørensen's outstanding achievements were probably only possible because he had the ability to find inspiration and new energy from many sources, not least through his profound and sincere love for nature and life. However, throughout the years, the marriage with Ellen Max Sørensen was more important than anything else for him, and their genuine and intimate life in common was the unfailing foundation for him and his work.

Max Sørensen was admired and respected in Denmark, in Europe and throughout the world to an extent which is rare for a Danish lawyer. Those who have known him, students, collaborators, colleagues and friends will retain the memory of him not only as an eminent lawyer but also as a warm-hearted man with high ideals and the profound belief that these ideals can be realized through indefatigable efforts. By his own life and work, Max Sørensen showed the best example.

Carl Aage Nørgaard

Do the rights set forth in the European Convention on Human Rights in 1950 have the same significance in 1975?

Report presented by
Max Sørensen
to the fourth international colloquy
about the European Convention on Human Rights

Rome, November 5-8, 1975

Introduction

The signature of the European Convention on Human Rights in Rome on 4 November 1950 was a historic landmark whose importance was obvious at the time, just as it is today. This product of full and intense discussion in the European Movement and the Consultative Assembly, finalized in the course of detailed work by experts and governmental representatives, came at a turning-point in European history. Its drafting and adoption were conditioned and favoured by an extraordinary concourse of political circumstances. The wrongs and depravities of the immediate past, combined with the threat to Western Europe of a new depotism explain the fervour and resolve of its authors and the welcome it received from public opinion.

If we ask today, after 25 years, whether the Convention's subsequent history has also been shaped by the unique circumstances which gave it birth, so that its importance has depended on later changes on the European political scene, the answer must be no. Despite the far-reaching political, economic and social changes in Western Europe, the Convention has preserved its initial significance.

There is nothing extraordinary in this. All the great historic declarations in the annals of human rights, by which we are still inspired, originated in similar momentary events. At other turning points in history the struggle against arbitrary authority also found expression in protests against wrongs and in demands for rights and freedoms that were being flouted. The declarations drawn up in such circumstances have survived the events that gave them birth. Their hold on the minds and their influence on the actions of men may be explained by the transcendental character of their affirmations. The rights and freedoms proclaimed were regarded as the expression of immutable values inherent in human nature, not dependent on political circumstances but valid for social life as a whole.

This is also true to a large extent of the 1948 Universal Declaration of Human Rights, immediate forerunner of, and a source of inspiration for, the European Convention of 1950. Whereas, however, the Declaration went beyond the framework of traditional rights and fredoms, also proclaiming economic, social and cultural

24

rights, the European Convention remained essentially within the narrower and firmer traditional structure. This difference may be explained not only by legal technicalities, such as the difficulty of formulating and applying the wider rights mentioned as individual or subjective rights, but also because of their dependence on material resources and the degree of social development.

Experience has confirmed this essential difference. In certain industrialised countries, the progress made in establishing economic and social rights has been such that the standards defined in 1948 have been left behind by subsequent developments and the initial expression is no longer adequate to the legitimate claims of individuals nowadays, whereas in other countries the economic and social rights proclaimed in the Universal Declaration are still a distant goal.

The civil and political rights, on the other hand, cannot be overtaken by social evolution. They still remain an aim to be achieved. This is equally true in Western Europe. What however distinguishes our countries from many others in the present-day world is that the achievement of traditional rights and freedoms is not subordinated to economic progress. The improvement of material conditions is not regarded as a prerequisite to respect for civil and political rights.

Recently, following the period of economic growth and the rise in the standard of living which in Europe marked the period that followed signature of the Convention in 1950, the cult of material values has been attacked and the economic structure of our industrial society challenged. However, such criticism is not directed against respect for individual rights and liberties and has indeed enjoyed their protection.

If we look towards the future the characteristic feature that we see is a gap between available material resources and the needs of a human society undergoing radical demographic change. It is obvious that new methods and practices will have to be found to control and master these economic and social factors. Despite all the uncertainty of Europe's future no less than of the world's, it is true to say that there seems to be no reason to challenge the values inherent in respect for individual rights and freedoms.

Far from any attempt to lessen the statement of rights drawn up in 1950, the need has since been felt to add to it by laying down rights which originally were regarded as secondary or which have since been seen as necessary because of unforeseen developments, especially in technology. Protocols nos. 1 and 4 to the Convention and the work programme drawn up by the Parliamentary Conference held in Vienna on 18-20 October, 1971 provide proof of this. The fact remains, however, that these additional rights, whether present or future, are only marginal to the original rights, which continue to form the essential nucleus. The significance of the right to life, the right to freedom of thought, opinion and expression and the other rights and freedoms laid down in the Convention remains today, as in the past, that of imposing minimum but absolute requirements on the exercise of public authority.

These introductory remarks to show that, for Europeans in the Council of Europe, the rights laid down in the European Convention of Human Rights retain in 1975 the significance they had when the Convention was drawn up in 1950, namely to express the essential principles binding on the State in the exercise of its authority over the individual.

This observation, however, is only a provisional and partial answer to the question with which this report is concerned. The rights embodied in the Convention are in many respects formulated in general and imprecise terms on whose meaning and scope opinions may differ. Has there been in this respect, over the last 25 years, any change in the conception and interpretation of the standards laid down in the Convention? That is the specific subject of the remarks which follow.

Part I
Evolutive interpretation methods

1. The Convention as an international treaty and enumeration of rights
One question arises before we start. Can the interpretation of a legal instrument vary as time passes? Is it possible for a provision of law to mean something different today from what it meant when it was adopted 25 years ago?

The European Convention on Human Rights, as a contractual instrument under international law, is subject to the *principles of interpretation applicable to international treaties in general.* In its judgment of 21 February 1975 (in the Golder case), the European Court of Human Rights, when considering what was the appropriate method for interpreting the Convention, opted for the rules on the subject in the Vienna Convention of 23 May 1969 on the Law of Treaties[1], Article 31, para 1 of which lays down the general principle that a treaty "shall be interpreted in good faith in accordance with the ordinary meaning to be given to the terms of the treaty in their context and in the lights of its object and purpose". The intentions of the Contracting Parties as revealed in the "travaux préparatoires" or by the circumstances in which the treaty was concluded are relevant only as a supplementary aid to interpretation laid down in the Vienna Convention that the accepted meaning of a term at the time a treaty is concluded does not necessarily take precedence over any new meaning which the same term may have acquired by the particular time of its application.

On the contrary, there are many cases in which the intention of the Contracting Parties is that the aim and purpose of a treaty run counter to any rigid and immutable fixing of legal rules, thus leaving the door open for possible changes in the social context in which the treaty is to be applied.[2] This is particularly true in the case of treaties which, like the European Convention, are full of general, imprecise notions frequently referring to non-legal standards of values such as "inhuman treatment", "within a reasonable time", "necessary in a democratic society" etc.

In one case where such notions had to be interpreted, the International Court of Justice accepted and applied this method of interpretation. Having been asked for a ruling on a matter relating to the legal status of the territory of Namibia, the Court expressed the following view on the appropriate interpretation of certain provisions of the League of Nations Covenant and the Mandate under which the Union of South Africa had been given the administration of the territory:

Mindful as it is of the primary necessity of interpreting an instrument in accordance with the intentions of the parties at the time of its conclusion, the Court is bound to take into account the fact that the concepts embodied in Article 22 of the Covenant – 'the strenuous conditions of the modern world' and 'the well-being and development' of the peoples concerned – were not static, but were by definition evolutionary, as also, therefore, was the concept of the 'sacred trust'. The parties to the Covenant must consequently be deemed to have accepted them as such. That is why, viewing the institutions of 1919, the Court must take into consideration the changes which have occurred in the supervening half-century, and its interpretation cannot remain unaffected by the subsequent development of law, through the Charter of the United Nations and by way of customary law. Moreover, an international instrument has to be interpreted and applied within the framework of the entire legal system prevailing at the time of the interpretation.[3]

To return to the European Convention on Human Rights as an international treaty, it may therefore be said that an interpretation which viewed certain of its terms as "evolutionary" concepts would not be in conflict with the generally accepted methods of interpretation.

This is the more clearly seen when the Convention is examined not only from the angle of international law but also from that of constitutional law. Such a view is borne out by the Convention's specific function, namely to provide rules, albeit in the form of an international instrument, for a field traditionally reserved to constitutional law, ie the fundamental rights of citizens as against the state. The formal status of the Convention in domestic law may admittedly vary from one Contracting State to another. Whether this status is identical with that of constitutional provisions or of a statute, or whether the Convention is not regarded as having any status of its own in national law, it has always been accepted that its ultimate purpose is the same as the *enumerations of fundamental rights* traditionally found in our constitutions. In most cases the Convention states some if not all of the rights and freedoms set forth in the constitutions of the Contracting Parties, although it gives them a new dimension in the form of an international obligation and collective guarantee.

In the majority of countries with a written constitution, its provisions are as a general rule interpreted in a flexible and dynamic manner. It is of course in the nature of a written constitution to promote stability. The procedure for amending and revising is more stringent than for ordinary legislation and its text is less readily adapted than a statutory text to the continual evolution of society.

28

By interpretation, however, it is possible to introduce the dynamic element capable of introducing some flexibility into the text, in order to meet new needs without jeopardising the desired stability of the constitution. To uphold and respect major principles in broad outline, while varying their specific effects according to social evolution, is the function of constitutional interpretation. This role is obvious in those countries where the judiciary, whether the ordinary courts or constitutional courts, verifies the conformity of laws and administrative decisions with the constitution, but it goes further than this.

We know from experience that it is mainly the definition of fundamental rights that is affected by their process of modification by court interpretation. Taking for example the changing meaning in the decisions of the United States Supreme Court, of concepts such as "equal protection of the laws" and "due process of law", or the evolution over the last century of rulings on racial questions, one cannot but be struck by the way in which the text of the constitution has been adapted to changes in social conditions and to new political and moral ideas.[4]

The same phenomenon may be observed in the decisions of the constitutional courts of certain European countries,[5] although the period covered by such decisions is shorter. A distinguished member of the Constitutional Court of the Federal Republic of Germany has spoken of "the constant task of adapting rigid constitutional standards effectively and dynamically to life's ever-changing needs".[6]

The contrast between a rigid text and flexible interpretation, thus regarded as a characteristic of national constitutions, is also apparent in the application of the Convention. The rigidity of the text is evident. Any amendment presupposes the agreement of all Contracting States, with the delays that such a process implies. For example, the Third Protocol, which involved no more than certain changes in the Commission's procedure and internal organisation, in particular the abolition of subcommissions, did not come into force until 1970, that is to say 7 years after its signature and 9 years after the Commission first submitted its proposal to the Committee of Ministers.[7] As for the provisions concerning the rights secured, there has been no amendment to the Convention during its first 25 years, although the inadequacy of certain of these provisions has become apparent. It is only by means of protocols, not requiring the consent of all the States Parties to the Convention and binding only on those which accept them, that the range of such rights has been extended. Without underestimating the importance of such extensions "in breadth", it must be conceded that this procedure hardly allows reinforcement "in depth" of the rights initially safeguarded by the Convention.

To conclude these remarks we may therefore say that, in the case of an instrument such as the European Convention on Human Rights, to use the method of interpretation of its provisions to introduce an element of dynamism and progress to keep pace with general social change is in keeping with generally accepted and recognized legal and judicial methods.

The question which now arises concerns the forms which such evolutive interpretations may take in actual application of the Convention.

2. What forms do new interpretations of the Convention take?

In the system set up to secure respect for the rights safeguarded by the Convention the responsibility for decisions entailing interpretation is vested in several different bodies. Most important of these decisions are the *judgments of the Court*. Although the Court has not so far had to decide a very large number of cases, its judgments have nevertheless made important contributions to the interpretation of the Convention. The cases submitted to the Court by decision of the Commission – and represent the great majority of cases heard by the Court – have been those involving important and difficult legal issues. In practice there has been a tendency on the Commission's part not to cite the respondent State before the Court if no question of principle was at stake.[8]

For the same reason, decisions taken by the *Committee of Ministers* on the basis of opinions formulated by the Commission are generally of only secondary interest, except that some of them concern States that have not recognised the Court's jurisdiction, so that the case cannot be referred to the Court however legally important it may be. In some such cases, the Commission's report, endorsed by the Committee of Ministers, contains matter that is bound to be of relevance to the development of the rights safeguarded.

As regards *decisions by the Commission on the admissibility of applica-*

tions it is generally recognised that they are taken in the exercise of a judicial function vested in the Commission. Because of their number and the diversity of the problems settled, they constitute a source of first importance, although it is in the nature of things that most of them, being to the effect that the application is inadmissible, do not provide any dynamic interpretations of the Convention.

On the other hand, one category of the Commission's reports is of special interest even though this is not always recognised. The reports in question are those that note that a *friendly settlement* has been reached. At first sight it may seem surprising that the friendly settlement of a dispute can help interpret the Convention. On closer inspection, however, such an end to a case is clearly relevant to the safeguard of the rights set forth in the Convention. A friendly settlement as provided for in Article 28 is not the outcome of a search for any area of agreement between the parties. The Commission's function is to seek a settlement "on the basis of respect for Human Rights as defined in this Convention" [Article 28 (b)].[9]

It follows that the Commission can neither seek nor approve a settlement which, while satisfying both parties, disregards a right secured by the Convention. A friendly settlement is therefore based on a legal opinion concerning the effect of the provisions invoked by the parties or considered as relevant by the Commission itself. This gives rise to an interpretation of the Convention which, while it does not rank as one of the traditional sources of law, is an important element in any realistic conception of the significance of the rights acknowledged.

It is true, on the other hand, that a government, when agreeing to such a friendly settlement, sometimes reserves its legal position by refusing to recognise that the Convention has been violated. Such an attitude however in no way diminishes the amends made to the victim in the case in point. The friendly settlement therefore accurately reflects the protection by individuals under the Convention, although by its very nature it cannot become part of case-law in the formal sense.

This is all the more true when the respondent government not only agrees to make full amends to the victim, but further declares its willingness to take the necessary steps to prevent any repetition of the decisions or events with which the application was concerned.

Legislative reforms, new administrative regulations or specific instructions to the authorities directly responsible are the main examples of such steps. It is clear that a settlement with such features reveals, by implication the relevant requirements of the Convention.

By way of illustration the following cases may be quoted:[10]

In the Alam and Singh cases (2991/66 and 2992/66) the United Kingdom Government introduced the Immigration Appeals Bill, subsequently enacted by parliament, to provide a new right of appeal.

In the Knechtel case (4115/69), the Commission's report notes that the United Kingdom Government decided to alter existing practice regarding a prisoner's right to consult a solicitor, and to authorise such consultation in all cases of alleged medical negligence by the prison authorities.

In connection with the Simon-Herold case (4340/69), the Austrian Ministry of Justice instructed all competent authorities to ensure that a prisoner of sound mind who had to be sent to hospital because of sickness or injury was not transferred to the closed ward of a psychiatric hospital.

A final example of more recent date is the friendly settlement in the case brought by Mr Gussenbauer, barrister, against Austria. The applicant had complained of the rules governing free legal aid, which in his submission imposed forced or compulsory labour on certain barristers in violation of Article 4 of the Convention. After the adoption of new legislation which met the requirements of the majority of barristers, and on the strength of certain assurances given by the government, the applicant declared himself satisfied and the Commission was able to endorse the settlement.[11]

One may go even further and consider the *arrangements* which are arrived at in the course of proceedings, or outside them, but which *do not amount to a friendly settlement* within the meaning af Article 28 of the Convention. In the De Becker case the Court was able to bring proceedings to an end and strike the case off its list after the Belgian Parliament had amended its legislation on forfeiture of civil rights by persons sentenced for crimes against the security of the state, thereby lifting the restrictions on freedom of expression which the Commission had considered to be incompatible with Article 10 of the Convention.[12]

Another example, in slightly different circumstances, may be found in the Pataki and Dunshirn cases (596/59 and 789/60). In view of the observations made by the representatives of the Commission in the course of negotiations for a friendly settlement, the Austrian Government proposed, and Parliament adopted, amendments to the code of criminal procedure designed to give full effect to the principle of "equality of arms" in criminal proceedings, in accordance with Article 6 of the Convention. For reasons of principle, the government submitted that it was unable to enter upon a friendly settlement with convicted prisoners serving their sentence; but in its report the Commission found that the new provisions, including those concerning trials already completed, would not be subject to the objections it had against proceedings under the former legislation. Subsequently the Committee of Ministers, following a proposal by the Commission, expressed its satisfaction at the new legislation introduced in Austria to ensure full application of the Convention, and decided that there was no reason to take any action on the cases under consideration.[13]

According to the traditional theory of sources of law, these examples can scarcely qualify as valid precedents. Despite this, they are of obvious value in helping to determine the meaning of provisions of the Convention.

3. The Convention's place in the world

The Convention is pre-eminently a European instrument. It encompasses all the European parliamentary democracies that are members of the Council of Europe and is not open to any other state. Nevertheless, its inspiration and purpose are wider than this. The Universal Declaration of Human Rights and the first draft of the United Nations Convenant on Civil and Political Rights and Freedoms were its main source, while some of the questions regulated by it are also the subject of international conventions concluded within the United Nations or its specialised agencies, such as ILO and UNESCO.

The application and interpretation of the Convention are therefore scarcely conceivable in European terms alone. True, the aim of the Convention from the outset was to protect the fundamental rights of the individual in Europe without awaiting further world-wide progress in this respect. There can thus be no question of lessening the degree of protection to match it with any lower level of protection offered by other international instruments, and progress towards more effective safeguards cannot be delayed in order not to outstrip progress in the rest of the world.

On the other hand, it is natural that progress achieved in specialised world-wide agencies or organisations should have repercussions on the application and interpretation of the European Convention, especially where its provisions cover the same ground as other international instruments.

It has been pointed out, for example, that the 1960 UNESCO Convention against Discrimination in Education is more explicit than Article 2 of the First Protocol to the European Convention in granting parents the right to have their children educated in schools other than those provided by the public authorities. Although this question arose in connection with the Belgian linguistic cases, neither the Commission nor the Court has expressed an opinion on the possible importance of the UNESCO Convention for interpretation of the Protocol.[14]

The Commission has, on the other hand, clearly stated its position regarding the relationship between the Convention and the instruments and case-law of the *International Labour Organisation*. On at least two points the European Convention contains provisions covering the same subjects as certain ILO conventions. Article 4 prohibits forced labour and Article 11 stipulates that everyone has the right to freedom of association, "including the right to form and to join trade unions for the protection of his interests".

With regard to interpretation of Article 4, the applicant in the Iversen case[15] referred to the ILO conventions on forced labour pointing out that they and the European Convention should be interpreted in the same way. In the Commission's decision on the admissibility of the application, four members of the majority expressed the following view:

... the concept of compulsory or forced labour cannot be understood solely in terms of the literal meaning of the words, and has in fact come to be regarded in international law and practice, as evidenced in part by the provisions and application of ILO Conventions and Resolutions on Forced Labour, as having

34

certain elements, and that it is reasonable, in the interpretation of Article 4, paragraph 2 of the Convention, to have due regard to those elements.[16]

It is true that the interpretation thus adopted did not extend the protection available to the applicant, and that the other members of the Commission, the other two members of the majority and the minority of four – expressed no opinion on this aspect of the problem. The passage quoted nevertheless foreshadowed the more positive attitude which the Commission was to adopt in later cases.

In connection with alleged violations of the trade union rights safeguarded in Article 11 of the Convention, the Commission again examined the relation between the European Convention and the International Labour Conventions. In case no 4125/69 the applicant complained of having been hampered in the free exercise of his functions as shop steward. The Irish Government, as respondent, argued that the right claimed was not protected by Article 11, which merely states that everyone has the right "to form and to join trade unions for the protection of his interests". The Commission considered however that, when interpreting the meaning and scope of freedom of association under Article 11 in relation to trade unions, it was necessary to have regard to the meaning given to this term in the ILO Convention of 1948 (no 87) concerning freedom of association and protection of the right to organise, Article 3 of which states the right of workers' and employers' organisations "to elect their representatives in full freedom" and "to organise their administration". In this particular case, however, the applicant had not exhausted the remedies available to him under Irish law for obtaining his rights in the national courts and his application was therefore declared inadmissible.[17]

The Commission's position was further clarified in two other cases brought by trade union organisations, namely the Belgian National Police Union (4464/70) and the Swedish Engine Drivers' Union (5614/72), both of which claimed that the right to protect the interests of their own members, irrespective of those of wider unions of public servants, had not been respected by the authorities designated by the state in the two countries to determine conditions of work and pay in the civil service. The issue at stake was whether those authorities had the right to recognise, for purpose of consultation and negotiation only those organisations which they considered as representative.

After adoption of the Commission's reports on 27 May 1974, both cases were referred to the Court. Without prejudging the outcome, it may be noted here that the Commission referred to certain ILO Conventions in order to clarify the meaning and scope of the notions of freedom of association and the right to form trade unions under Article 11. It pointed out that these conventions had been ratified by a large number of states, including almost all Parties to the European Convention on Human Rights, and that they reflected widely accepted labour law standards. They should therefore not be ignored in any interpretation of Article 11 if the European Convention was not to fall behind progress in international labour law.[18]

4. Evolution through the case-law and practice of the Contracting States

It is a well-known fact that the Contracting States have adopted different methods, in accordance with their own constitutional practices, to give effect to the Convention in their domestic systems of law, and this is not the place to re-open discussion on that subject.[19] Whatever the formal status of the Convention in each Contracting State, there can be no doubt that it is primarily before national administrative and judicial authorities that we must seek respect for the rights and freedoms embodied in the Convention. The safeguards provided in the form of proceedings before the Commission and Court have only secondary importance. The principle in Article 26 regarding the exhaustion of domestic remedies is the most important expression of this. The Court has, moreover, expressly acknowledged elsewhere the subsidiary nature of the international machinery of collective enforcement established by the Convention.[20] It follows that the authorities of the Contracting States, above all the national courts, will frequently have to interpret provisions of the Convention even in cases where those concerned do not consider it necessary or desirable to refer the matter to the organs set up by the Convention.

Since the Convention makes no provision for any procedure similar to that under Article 177 of the Treaty establishing the European Economic Community, national courts are denied the power of referring to the European Court of Human Rights for preliminary interpretations. It may therefore happen that, although not obliged to do so by any general international case-law or any specific preliminary ruling, a national court applies a provision of the Convention, using a forward-looking interpretation.[21] One of the most striking examples of this is the way in which certain German courts have applied Article 8 of the Convention, on respect for family life, to prevent the expulsion of an alien in circumstances which would lead to separation of the family.[22]

It has even been argued that the Convention encourages national courts to be more generous than its own provisions require. Article 60 specifies that the Convention cannot limit any of the rights and freedoms which may be ensured under national laws. Over and above that, it has been claimed, the Convention does not prevent the national court from placing a broad interpretation on it, and national decisions based on the Convention have in fact proved to be bolder than are, or indeed can be, those of the Commission and Court, for they, as international organs, are obliged to observe a degree of caution.[23]

While it is true that the decisions taken by the Commission and Court on controversial matters are often somewhat cautious – which may be explained up to a point by the fact that recognition of their powers under Articles 25 and 46 is optional – the fact remains that they frequently find inspiration and support in the practice of member states.

An analysis of such practice in a specific field may serve not only to define the limits of one of the rights safeguarded, but also to justify a broad and liberal interpretation. It has been rightly pointed out that such a method of interpretation is preferable to the traditional method in that it makes it possible to keep pace with progress in national legal institutions and standards and encourages interaction between national law and the Convention.[24]

This interaction is a complex and subtle proces. It is in the national context that the new ideas which give rise to law reform are born and develop. The influence of one European country and another and European discussion tend to promote uniformity in currents of thought and reform trends, but it cannot be denied that there is often little consistency in the changes they bring about in legislation and legal institutions. The European organs responsible for applying the Convention cannot blaze the trail, but neither should they be content merely to bring up the rear. The question sometimes arises whether a government which made no reservations under Article 64 at the time of ratifying the Convention can legitimately contend that its legislation as it existed at that time should be regarded as satisfying the requirements of the Convention. The Commission and the Court have never accepted this view.

In the Delcourt case, the Belgian provisions dating from 1815 concerning the role of the Procureur Général at the Court of Cassation, were examined by the Court, from this standpoint, although a secondary issue. The Court found, firstly, that the age of a rule of national law could not justify a failure to comply with the present requirements of international law, although it might, in certain circumstances, provide supporting evidence that there had been no such failure. In view of the wide measure of agreement in professional circles and public opinion that the prevailing system was satisfactory, the Court found that the applicant had not been denied a fair trial.[25]

In more general terms, the Austrian Government submitted, in the Neumeister case, that the system of criminal procedure which had necessitated the applicant's long period of remand during the preliminary investigation was common to all continental states and satisfied the principles of the Convention both at the time of its ratification and at the time when the events under consideration took place.[26] In its judgment the Court did not accept this argument, although it appears to have agreed that the system itself could not be criticised as failing to comply with the Convention.[27]

Although no definite conclusion emerges from this case regarding the issue under consideration, governments have on other occasions recognised that the Convention required them to amend provisions of law which were in force at the time of ratification and whose conformity with the Convention had not then been questioned. We have already mentioned that the Pataki and Dunshirn cases prompted the Austrian Government to amend the provisions of its Code of Criminal Procedure regarding the functions of the public prosecutor at the courts of appeal.[28] Another long-standing provision of the same code has been amended subsequent to the Commission's examination of the Vampel case (no 4465/70). This was Article 180 (2), which required remand in custody in all cases where the offence concerned carried a minimum penalty of 10 years' imprisonment.[29] Many similar examples might be quoted.

There can be no denying, therefore, that the degree of commitment by Contracting States is not tied to the state of their legislation at the time of ratification. Interpretation of the Convention cannot be confined to presumptions as to what intentions states would have wished to indicate if the question had been put to them at the time. Indeed, the trend may be quite the opposite. National developments may help to raise the level of commitment even above what was generally acceptable at the outset. What is important in this respect is that such developments should be sufficiently widespread and not limited to a few states. As a distinguished member of the Court has remarked, the homogeneity which exists among European states enables a fairly high standard to be set, but it is not enough to secure total equality. While the organs of the Convention cannot ignore existing differences, their interpretation of the Convention need not necessarily remain static. It can be flexible and become stricter as the harmonisation of legal systems progresses.[30]

Part II
The evolution of specific rights

Having devoted the first part of this report to certain aspects of methods of interpretation whereby the Convention may be applied in a forward-looking spirit, attention should now be focused on the specific rights defined in the Convention, in order to see what new significance they may have acquired over the last 25 years.

From the great mass of decisions taken and opinions stated by the organs of the Convention and of Member States, it seems possible to discern certain general outlines and predominant trends. Given the Convention's ideological foundation and practical objective, it may be assumed that evolution will be guided by a concern for humanity, equality and certainty as to the law. This assumption is in fact borne out by a detailed study of the change that has taken place.[31]

Some of the features will be left aside in this report, which must concentrate on what would appear to be essential. It is our aim moreover not to encroach upon the subject-matter of the rapporteurs who are to deal with the evolution of certain specific rights or with acceptable restrictions on the exercise of freedom. Finnally, with regard to the right to respect for private and family life under Artickle 8 of the Convention, we refer readers to the thorough study by Mr Torkel Opsahl submitted at the Brussels Symposium in 1970.[32] We shall merely reiterate some of his conclusions.

1. Humanitarianism as a factor in change

Humanitarian considerations are not merely entrenched in the general objectives of the Convention and its provisions as a whole, but more specifically in *Article 3,* which forbids torture and also *"inhuman or degrading"* treatment or punishment.

A historical interpretation of these words might have led to conferring a fairly narrow meaning on them. The fact that the authors of the Universal Declaration and the European Convention felt it necessary to ban such practices in a modern enumeration of human rights is due, without any doubt, to the terrible experiences under the Nazi regime. It was hoped to rule out any possibility of further such experiences.

The prohibition is however expressed in fairly general terms which do not necessarily refer exclusively to the practices of the concentration camps and racial persecution. The wording of Article 3 is a classic example of vague phraseology, which may be diversely interpreted according to current attitudes in society.

In its decisions, the Commission has therefore had to steer a course between two hazards: on the one hand, a broad interpretation going beyond what the Contracting Parties would be prepared to accept, and on the other, a narrow interpretation that would make the provision utterly meaningless in the normal conditions prevailing in Western Europe.

Very frequently, the Commission receives applications alleging ill-treatment, resort to violence, sometimes even a degree of brutality, on the part of police or prison staff. Nevertheless, the Commission has had to acknowledge that the use of force may become necessary in certain circumstances and that not all ill-treatment is necessarily inhuman or degrading.[33]

On the other hand, the Commission has used a very broad interpretation of Article 3 to deal with a problem which is not specifically covered by any provision of the Convention, namely the *expulsion and extradition of aliens.* It might have been thought that an application on this subject would have to be declared inadmissible as being incompatible with the Convention, which does not lay down any conditions for extradition or expulsion. The Commission felt however that the deportation of an alien to a particular country could, in exceptional cases, raise the question whether such expulsion constituted "inhuman treatment" within the meaning of Article 3. This would be so, for example, when there was good reason to fear that in the state to which he had been deported the individual might be exposed to treatment prohibited by the Convention.[34] The Commission confirmed this view with regard to extradition to one particular country by stating that the question of inhuman treatment might arise if "owing to the very nature of the regime of that country or to a particular stituation in that country, basic human rights, such as are guaranteed by the Convention, might be either grossly violated or entirely suppressed".[35]

In the great majority of cases the Commission has found that the circumstances did not justify such a view. Such an interpretation of Article 3 has however in certain cases enabled the Secretary of the Commission to make unofficial approaches to the governments challenged so that they shall delay deportation or extradition until the case has been examined by the Commission. This has incidentally made it possible on occasion to reach a settlement out of court.

In one of the rare cases where the application was declared admissible in this respect, the respondent government agreed, through the friendly settlement procedure, to award considerable compensation to the victim's widow. The case concerned a Moroccan officer who, after taking part in an abortive attempt on the life of the king, had fled to Gibraltar where he requested political asylum. After a short period of detention he was handed over to the Moroccan authorities. He was condemned to death by a Moroccan court and executed shortly afterwards. Although the United Kingdom Government declared that the friendly settlement did not imply an admission on its part to having violated the Convention, the friendly settlement would scarecely have been possible without a broad interpretation of Article 3.[36]

Like "inhuman treatment", the notion of *"degrading treatment"* is open to a liberal interpretation guided by the evolution of ideas and values generally accepted in society. The two notions are very akin, moreover, and the Commission has rarely had occasion to focus special attention on the meaning of the term "degrading".

Such an occasion did arise however in the examination of the cases concerning the immigration of East African Asians to the United Kingdom. A preliminary report on some of these cases was adopted by the Commission in December 1973 and communicated to the Committee of Ministers. For the time being, pending publication of this report, analysis can be based only on the decision of admissibility, which does however contain certain points of the greatest interest.

The applicants, of Asian origin, were United Kingdom citizens and holders of British passports. They complained that the United Kingdom Government had refused to allow them to enter the country or settle there permanently, at a time when they were unable either to remain in their former country of residence or to enter any other country. They alleged that this refusal and the legislation on which it was based placed them in a situation of inferiority because of their race, and were thus discrimination contrary to the Convention as well as being degrading treatment within the meaning of Article 3. In its defence, the United Kingdom Government argued that it had not ratified the Fourth Protocol, Article 3 of which secured the right of any person to enter the territory of the state of which he was a national, and that the ban on discrimination contained in Article 14 of the Convention referred only to the rights set forth in the Convention and in the Protocols, forming an integral part of it.

In its decision of 10 October 1970 declaring the applications admissible, the Commission expressed the opinion that, quite apart from Article 14, discrimination might, under certain conditions, in itself constitute degrading treatment within the meaning of Article 3. The Commission considered that publicly to single out one group of persons for differential treatment based on race might in certain circumstances, constitute a special form of affront to human dignity. Consequently, differential treatment of this kind applied on the basis of race might be capable of constituting degrading treatment in circumstances where differential treatment on some other ground, such as language, would raise no such question.[37]

While these statements are not necessarily the last word on the subject, they nevertheless open up the prospect that Article 3 may assume greater importance, and even new significance, among the rights secured by the Convention.

The humanitarian views behind this new trend are also at the origin of the broader conception of family life which is emerging in the Commission's decisions on *Article 8* of the Convention. As pointed out at the Third International Symposium on the Convention, held in Brussels in 1970,[38] the meaning of the term "*family*" depends on sociological factors which vary in different periods of history and types of civilisation. The interpretation of the term as it appears in the Convention must therefore reflect the diversity of the social and cultural characteristics of the family's role at different times and in different parts of Europe, and perhaps even beyond Europe in that persons from other parts of the world settle in our continent, and the Convention is applicable in certain non-European territories of the Contracting States.

In the application of Article 8 there has been a tendency to recognise that the rights mentioned in paragraph 2 should be enjoyed by both parents, not only the mother in relations with an "illegitimate" child. It is obvious also that there are many circumstances in which public authorities must interfere in such relations in order to protect the interests of the child. Such interference may perhaps be justified as a legitimate restriction under Article 8 (2).

The changes in habits and customs which are a feature of our times raise the question whether official marriage is the only basis on which a couple can conduct family life eligible for protection under Article 8. While the problem does not yet appear to have been decided one way or the other by the organs of the Convention, legal writers have occasionally advocated a liberal interpretation for the benefit of couples who are living together without having contracted a formal marriage.[39]

There is no doubt that the human values at stake in such cases may be just as worthy of protection under the Convention as in the case of marriages sanctioned by an official certificate. This is a subject however in which the above-mentioned interaction between national law and the Convention is of special importance.

43

2. The establishment of equality

A superficial view would suggest that the Convention precludes any inequality in the enjoyment of the rights safeguarded. After all, does not Article 1 stipulate that the rights and freedoms defined in Section I of the Convention shall be secured "to everyone" within the jurisdiction of the Contracting Parties?

Nevertheless, the problem is not so simple. In the first place, the restrictions authorised by certain clauses of the Convention may entail inequalities, although these should never be applied so as to cause discrimination contrary to Article 14. Secondly, there has been much discussion of whether it is not implicit that certain categories of persons are not qualified to claim protection under the Convention. The question is whether certain "*inherent limitations*" exist in addition to the restrictions expressly authorised. Such limitations might apply for example to prisoners, servicemen, minors and the mentally handicapped.

Protection of the rights of such persons was the subject of a report by Mr Pierre Mertens examined at the Parliamentary Conference held in Vienna in October 1971. On that occasion, however, the discussion was more concerned with the advisability or necessity of new measures than with how texts already in force were being applied.[40]

The case-law of the Convention organs offers much food for thought. The detailed facts will be covered in the special study of restrictions on which Mr Jacobs is to report to this colloquy. For the present we may simply indicate that, broadly speaking, this case-law shows an increasingly marked reserve with regard to the notion of inherent limitations.

The question has arisen above all with reference to *prisoners*.[41] To begin with, the Commission seems to have had recourse to this notion to justify restrictions, particulary on the private and family life of prisoners. In the "vagrancy" cases the Commission referred to its own previous decision that inspection of the correspondence of a prisoner serving sentence could be regarded as an inherent feature of deprivation of liberty. In the case under consideration, which entailed detention for mere vagrancy as opposed to a criminal sentence, the Commission considered however that such inspection was not justified by the cause of detention. The Court dismissed the notion

44

of an inherent limitation. On the other hand it felt that Article 8 (2) was a sufficient basis for imposing the restrictions.[42]

The problem arose again in the Golder case. While serving a term of imprisonment the applicant bad been refused permission to consult a solicitor with a view to bringing an action for libel against a prison officer. The respondent government had advanced the doctrine of inherent limitations, but this time the Commission clearly refuted it: "... restrictions involved in imprisonment have more to do with what is at any time regarded as desirable and reasonable than with any 'inherent' feature. Consequently, Article 5 does not offer in principle any more solid basis for introducing 'inherent limitations' of the regular human rights of prisoners laid down elsewhere in the Convention than for their total denial to detainees in general".[43]

The Court for its part does not seem to have wished to rule out the existence of any limitation accepted by implication. It reiterated, however, a statement made in a previous judgment that national rules on the enjoyment of one of the rights safeguarded by the Convention should never jeopardise the substance of that right. It held that its function was not "to elaborate a general theory of the limitations admissible in the case of convicted prisoners" and simply concluded that, in the given circumstances, the applicant should have been authorised to consult a solicitor with a view to instituting legal proceedings.[44]

The tendency in the case-law of the Convention organs is thus to secure to prisoners equal enjoyment of rights with other persons. This trend is, moreover, completely in line with the evolution of ideas and practices with regard to prison policy. A convicted prisoner is regarded less and less as a "prisoner" and more and more as a "detained citizen".

Recently the question arose whether the Convention applied to *members of the armed forces,* especially where military discipline was concerned. When the Convention was being drafted this problem does not seem to have received attention. Otherwise reservations similar to those made by the French Government when ratifying the Convention in 1974 would have been formulated to make Articles 5 and 6 inapplicable to problems of discipline in the armed forces.

In view of the existing wording of the text, however, the question has been raised whether any limitations are inherent in the special status of servicemen. In the cases of the "five Netherlands soldiers" (5100-02/71, 5354/72 and 5370/72) the Commission discussed this matter in its report of 19 July 1974. Arguing from Article 1 of the Convention, it expressed the opinion that there was nothing in the general character of that provision that justified distinguishing between different categories of persons such as ordinary citizens and servicemen in such a way that the Convention would not apply to the latter.

The case has now been brought before the Court. Pending its judgment one is bound to observe that the general tendency in our countries in favour of granting "citizens in uniform" equal rights with other citizens cannot but influence the interpretation and application of the Convention.

Equality is not however an absolute value. Equal treatment presupposes comparability, and how is one to decide whether two situations are comparable? What criterion should be applied to decide whether they are equal and can be given equal treatment? Does equality not presuppose that what is unequal should be treated unequally? All these questions touch the very heart of the problem of discrimination.

Article 14 requires that the enjoyment of the rights and freedoms set forth in the Convention shall be secured *without discrimination*. The French text uses an even more stringent phrase: "sans distinction aucune". Interpretation of this article has undergone a remarkable evolution in the course of which it has acquired a more specific but also more qualified meaning than at the time the Convention was drafted.

Initially, the Commission held the view that the reference to other rights and freedoms safeguarded in the Convention meant that violation of Article 14 presupposed violation of another provision of the Convention. Discrimination could therefore be an aggravating circumstance of some other violation but not a violation in itself.[45] It was not until it came to examine the Belgian linguistic cases that the Commission revised this opinion. It held that in all cases where other articles failed to give a precise definition of the rights they secured, leaving states either a margin of discretion, the option of imposing certain restrictions or a choice of means to give effect to the right, Article 14 could have independent significance if such latitude was used in a discriminatory manner. The Court concurred on this point, stating that "a measure which in itself is in conformity with the requirements of the article enshrining the right or freedom in question may however infringe this article when read in conjunction with Article 14, for the reason that it is of a discriminatory nature".[46]

Analysing further the problem of equality, the Court, again in agreement with the Commission, remarked that, despite the very general wording of the French version, Article 14 did not forbid all differences in treatment in the exercise of the rights and freedoms recognised. Diverse situations or problems frequently called for different legal solutions, and certain legal inequalities were in any case intended only to correct inequalities in fact. In trying to establish criteria to determine whether or not a given difference in treatment is legitimate, the Court made the following statement, which is one of the most remarkable passages in its case-law:

... the Court, following the principles which may be extracted from the legal practice of a large number of democratic States, holds that the principle of equality of treatment is violated if the distinction has no objective and reasonable justification. The existence of such a justification must be assessed in relation to the aim and effects of the measure under consideration, regard being had to the principles which normally prevail in democratic societies. A difference of treatment in the exercise of a right laid down in the Convention must not only pursue a legitimate aim; Article 14 is likewise violated when it is clearly etstablished that there is no reasonable relationship of proportionality between the means imployed and the aim sought to be realised.[47]

In another case (2299/64, Grandrath), the Commission reached a similar conclusion,[48] so that this new interpretation of Article 14 is now firmly established. It follows that the criteria used for determining whether differential treatment is legitimate or not are general and not very precise guidelines. The evolution observed will therefore have the effect of increasing the importance of the procedures laid down for supervising application of the Convention by the Contracting States.

3. The concern for certainty as to the law
Like all its forerunners, the enumeration of rights and freedoms in the European Convention is permeated with the principle of what may be called "security under the law" (sécurité juridique). In order

to be permissible, restrictions on rights and freedoms must be prescribed by law, the independence and impartiality of the courts must be respected and criminal laws may not be made retroactive. Given these fundamental axioms however, one may wonder just how far the effects of the principle should make themselves felt in judicial and administrative practice. In this respect the text of the Convention is sometimes open to different interpretations and it is of interest to see how far developments over the last 25 years have helped consolidate the notion of security under the law.

One of the first areas where the problem has arisen is that of *criminal proceedings*. The minimum safeguards for accused persons under Articles 5, 6 and 7 are fairly specific and detailed, but it is certain that the definition is not exhaustive. Furthermore, the requirement that a case should have a "fair hearing" by the competent court, in other words the notion of the "fair trial", is open to divergent interpretations.

The organs of the Convention have most frequently had to express opinions on the situation of the accused vis-à-vis the prosecuting authority. The Commission considers that the concept of a fair trial requires that the two parties to the trial should be placed on an equal footing, and has adopted for the purposes of the Convention the concept of *"equality of arms"* used in the terminology of certain national systems of criminal procedure. The problem was raised in very clear terms in the Pataki and Dunshirn cases, in which the applicants contended that Article 6 of the Convention had been violated in that the Public Prosecutor, but not the accused or their counsel, had been present at the hearings and deliberations of the Vienna Court of Appeal concerned with their cases. The Commission held that "what is generally called 'the equality of arms', that is the procedural equality of the accused with the public prosecutor, is an inherent element of a fair trial«. In the circumstances of the case it was not possible to establish with certainty whether the public prosecutor had taken an active part in the deliberations of the court. But the mere fact of his presence, which afforded him an opportunity of influencing the members of the court without the accused or their counsel having any silimar opportunity, constituted an inequality which, in the Commission's opinion, was incompatible with the notion of a fair trial.[49]

The Committee of Ministers agreed with this opinion and, as already mentioned, the Austrian Code of Criminal Procedure was amended accordingly. The Court has adopted a similar attitude. Ruling on another case, it referred to the "principle of 'equality of arms' which the Commission, in several decisions and opinions, has rightly stated to be included in the notion of fair trial".[50]

In *civil law disputes*, too, security under the law demands a fair trial, although this notion does not have the same substance in proceedings where the Public Prosecutor does not appear as adversary or the private party. The essential point in civil actions is relatively easy access to an impartial court. Article 6 does not expressly stipulate a right of access, and indeed one government recently contested the existence of such a right. In the Golder case the applicant was refused permission to consult a solicitor with a view to taking civil action against a prison officer for libel. In the Commission's view, which was confirmed by the Court, such a hindrance to institution of the proposed action constituted a violation of Article 6 (1) of the Convention.

The Court considered in fact that the *right of access to a court* was inherent in the right laid down in Article 6 (1). It stated that this interpretation was not an extensive one placing new obligations on the Contracting States. Its interpretation nevertheless deserves our attention as a significant contribution to strengthening security under the law, in accordance with the aims of the Convention.

In the same context it is interesting to note that the Court also took account of the principle of the rule of law, mentioned in the preamble to the Convention and to the Statute of the Council of Europe. In civil matters, it held, one could scarely conceive of the rule of law without there being a possibility of having access to the courts. In support of this interpretation it further observed that the principle whereby a civil claim must be capable of being submitted to a judge ranked as one of the universally "recognised" fundamental principles of law, as did the principle of international law which forbade the denial of justice.[51]

As a whole and in its detailed reasoning, then, this recent contribution to case-law on the Convention reinforces the Convention's role as a guardian of security under the law.

A third topic which occupies an important place in the case-law on the Convention is interpretation of the words "*civil rights and obligations*" ("droits et obligations de caractère civil") in Article 6 (1) of the Convention. It is for the determination of such rights and obligations and of criminal charges that the right of access to a court is laid down. If the dispute does not enter into either of these two categories then access to the courts, ie the right to a court decision, is not secured. This might for example occur in matters of administrative law or public law in general: hence the importance of the problem.

In its usual meaning the wording of the Convention in both languages is confusing and the "travaux préparatoires" do not remove the ambiguity.[52] The organs of the Convention, especially the Commission, have endeavoured to define categories of dispute not covered by the article, by using a case-by-case approach rather than a comprehensive one. There is no need here to follow these decisions in every detail;[53] all that is necessary is to pick out certain essential points. The Commission has considered Article 6 to be inapplicable in matters relating to taxation, social security contributions and benefits, entry to civil service posts, admission to law examinations and the bar and various disciplinary procedures.

In the Ringeisen case, the Commission attempted to set out its ideas in more general terms. It pointed out that one characteristic of modern European states was that many private activities were dependent on official permits determining the rights and obligations of citizens of those concerned. This was the case, for example, with regard to the use of land, the exercise of certain professions, the performance of certain contracts and even certain day-to-day activities. It was only rarely, if at all, that the decisions on such matters were taken in circumstances which satisfied Article 6. Most of these decisions were administrative ones, and while attempts were made in all member countries to establish procedures for supervising the lawfulness of administrative decisions, the methods varied greatly from country to country and could not be squared with the procedural requirements of Article 6 in all disputes between individuals and public authorities.[54]

The case in point concerned approval by an Austrian administrative commission of a contract for the purchase of agricultural land. Under the relevant law on real property transactions the withholding of approval voided the contract. In these circumstances the Court, following the opinion expressed by the minority of the Commission, ruled that Article 6 did apply, in that it covered all proceedings the result of which was decisive for private rights and obligations. This was exactly the position in the case under consideration. Although it was applying rules of administrative law, the administrative commission's decision was to be decisive in the civil law relations betwen the seller and the buyer.[55]

This judgment is thus an interesting stage in the creation of ever greater security under the law. No doubt this is not the Court's last word on the subject, and it has solved only a small part of the problem. It did not concur with the more radical opinion expressed by the minority of the Commission as described by the principal delegate before the Court, who had said that civil rights and obligations embraced "those rights and obligations which are established by law for the individual in his relations with other persons or with the state and its various agencies in such matters as personal status, property, contract and fault. To give a simple example, the compulsory acquisition of private property for public purpose would, in this view, involve civil rights and obligations".[56]

On the other hand, the delegate of the Commission did not claim that administrative bodies had themselves to observe the procedural requirement of Article 6 (1), merely that there must in the whole process be a judicial element of fair hearing.[57]

For its part, the Court did not adopt this very free interpretation of Article 6. It merely observed that the administrative commission in question was a tribunal within the meaning of the article and that the rule of impartiality laid down therein had not been disregarded.[58]

This reveals the interplay of opinions in the evolutionary process from which progress emerges. As a guide for future evolution, the view expressed by the minority of the Commission in the Ringeisen case is most constructive and attractive. Is it possible to say at the present juncture, that Article 6 of the Convention has already acquired a new meaning? There is no easy answer to this question, and that in itself shows that attitudes are no longer rigid.

Part III
Duties of individuals?

Rights and duties are complementary. The duties of one group correspond to the rights of another. This philosophical, moral and legal axiom is frequently disregarded and is only rarely given adequate expression in declarations of human rights.[59]

The Universal Declaration of 1948 proclaims that "Everyone has duties to the community in which alone the free and full development of his personality is possible" (Article 29, para 1). It is the individual's duties towards the community to which he belongs that are stated here, not his duties towards other members of the community as individuals. The second paragraph stipulates that, in the exercise of his rights and freedoms, the individual is subject to such limitations as are determined by law "for the purpose of securing due recognition and respect for the rights and freedoms of others". The stress is therefore on the restrictions limiting the rights of the individual himself, not on the contributions he must make, by actions or omissions, to securing the rights of others.

The European Convention is plainly concerned with rights, admittedly subject to certain restrictions, and not with the corresponding duties. This may be explained by the Convention's specific purpose, which was to protect individuals against wrongful and arbitrary action by public authorities, not to regulate the relations of individuals to each other. The duties corresponding to the rights of individuals devolve upon states. It is true that Article 1 may be interpreted as meaning that states should ensure that individual rights are respected not only by the public authorities but also by other protagonists in society ("the High Contracting Parties shall secure" – in French »reconnaissent« – "to everyone within their jurisdiction the rights and freedoms ..."). On the other hand, proceedings under the Convention, whether for applications by states (Article 24) or by individuals (Article 25), are directed entirely against Contracting Parties, in other words states. The possibility of holding anyone else responsible for infringements of individual rights does not exist.

This was the starting point for the theoretical debate which has developed around this subject over the years, on the basis of the theory and practice of certain national legal systems in which the fundamental rights defined in the constitution are considered to be enforceable by the individuals concerned against private persons as well as authorities. In German terminology this phenomenon is known as "Drittwirkung".[60]

Where the provisions of the European Convention are concerned, one theory considers that they should be acknowledged to have this effect nationally, while admitting that the problem is different as regards the procedures established under the Convention. The organs of the Convention have not had the occasion to express any view on this distinction. Nevertheless, the Commission has consistently ruled that applications directed against individuals are inadmissible as being incompatible with the Convention, the Commission not being competent *ratione personae* to deal with such applications. This is the case, for example, if the applicant alleges that his counsel in a civil or criminal case failed to defend him properly, with the result that he was deprived of a fair hearing.

To this initial case-law the Commission had added a subsequent decision concerning defence counsel appointed by the courts ex officio, in the following terms:

... an examination of the case as it has been submitted does not disclose any grounds on which the alleged conduct of the lawyer who was appointed ex officio for the Applicant's defence could exceptionally entail the responsibility of the Government ... under the Convention.[61]

The reasoning behind this statement appears to be that, by allowing the trial to continue without taking action against the lawyer's negligence, the court could have made the Contracting State internationally liable. In actual fact therefore, there is no question of any duties on the individual under the Convention.

A further contribution to case-law on the general problem of the individual's duties has been made by the Commission in recent cases concerning *trade union rights*. In situations where applicants, both natural and artificial persons, have alleged violations of their rights under Article 11 of the Convention by public bodies acting as employers, not in the exercise of state authority, the Commission has accepted that the state could have been responsible for such violations. After an initial indication of this possibility in a decision declaring an application inadmissible on other grounds,[62] the Commission expressed this opinion more clearly in the two reports adopted on 27 May 1974.[63] The Commission agreed that the Convention fundamentally guaranteed traditional freedoms in relation to the state as the holder of public power. This did not, however, imply that the state could not be obliged to protect individuals through appropriate measures against some forms of interference by other individuals, groups or organisations.. While these could not themselves, under the Convention, be held responsible for any such acts which were in breach of the Convention, the state might, under certain circumstances, be responsible for them.[64]

As these two cases have now been submitted to the Court, it is premature to draw any firm conclusions from the Commission's opinion. It may however be noted that an earlier attitude hitherto considered as firmly established has been modified in a manner which may give new meaning to several provisions of the Convention. The trend takes account of certain structural innovations in contemporary society. More and more the state is having to share its power with non-state organisations and institutions. The rights and freedoms of the individual are threatened as much by the actions of these newcomers to the political, economic and social scene as by those of the state authorities. To declare the state responsible for resultant violations of rights is bound to raise new problems, for the public authorities are not fully in control of these new centres of power and influence. Solving these problems will not be easy, but what matters is that a new tendency should become apparent to strengthen the European Convention as an instrument in the service of individual rights and freedoms.

Conclusion

The European Convention on Human Rights is a living legal instrument. This is the first conclusion which results from our brief study. Its provisions are capable of being interpreted in such a way as to keep pace with social change. The positions adopted by the organs responsible for applying the Convention furnish many examples of this.

Nevertheless, this change is moderate. That is the second conclusion to be drawn. There is nothing startling in the decisions of the Commission and Court. We find few bold rulings of the kind sometimes handed down by higher national courts of certain countries, which have made or even reversed the law in such a way as to go down in national political history.

The organs of the Convention have thus remained faithful to their international mission. As an international treaty, the Convention rests in the final analysis on the consent of the Contracting States. It can be denounced, and the powers of its organs depend essentially on specific acknowledgment by those states.

It follows that the Convention is not designed to promote social reform, but it can be used both to preserve what has been achieved and also to express a newly emerging consensus and bring states which are lagging behind into line with a general trend in ideas and institutions in Europe. In this sense it may be instrumental in bringing about reform in the Contracting States. If its organs make common cause with currents of opinion that favour humanity, the rule of law and freedoms, they can so handle it as to give ever fuller effect to the ideas which inspired it.

The new meanings acquired by the Convention on a number of detailed points are thus in keeping with its unchanging significance.

Notes

1. Eur. Court of H. R., Golder Case, judgment of 21 February 1975, § 29.
2. Rudolf Bernhardt; "Die Auslegung völkerrechtlicher Verträge", 1963, especially pp 163 et seq. ("Die allgemeine Lebens- und Sozialordnung").
3. I. C. J. Report 1971, p 31.
4. See, for example, Henry J. Abraham: Freedom and the Court, New York 1967, especially pp 242 et seq.
5. Peter Häberle: Zeit und Verfassung, Zeitschrift für Politik, 1974, pp 111-136; Ulrich Scheuner in Staatslexikon, Bd. 8, 1963, p. 126 ("Verfassungsrecht und Verfassungsauslegung"); Felix Ermacora: Allgemeine Staatslehre 197), Bd. 2, pp 800 et seq.

6. Theodor Ritterspach in Jahrbuch des Öffentlichen Rechts, NF Bd. 20, 1971, p 109.

7. Yearbook of the European Convention on Human Rights, vol 4, 1961, p 104.

8. Sture Petrén: La Saisine de la Cour Européenne par la Commission Européenne des Droits de l'Homme, in Mélanges offerts à Polys Modinos, 1968, pp 233 et seq.

9. François Monconduit: La Commission Européenne des Droits de l'Homme, Leyden 1965, pp 375-85; Jean Raymond: Comment s'exerce la fonction de conciliation de la Commission Européenne des Droits de l'Homme, HRJ vol II, 1969, pp 259-66; Henri Rolin, HRJ vol VI, 1973, pp 739-44; J. A. Frowein, in Privacy and Human Rights, Manchester, 1973, pp 284-290.

10. European Commission on Human Rights (A. B. McNulty), Stock-taking on the Convention, DH (74) 6, pp 20 et seq.

11. W. Peukert in Grundrechte, Europäische Grundrechte-Zeitschrift (EuGRZ), 2.Jg.Heft 3, 7 February 1975, p 56, cf Stocktaking, DH (74) 6, pp 53 et seq.

12. Publications of the European Court of Human Rights, Series A, judgment of 27 March 1962, De Becker Case, cf Series B, 1962, pp 188 et seq.

13. Yearbook, vol 6, 1963, pp 715 et seq. For further examples see Stock-taking, DH (74) 6, pp 27 et seq.

14. Torkel Opsahl in Privacy and Human Rights, Proceedings of the Brussels Colloquy of 1970, Manchester, 1973, pp 182 et seq.

15. Case 1468/62, Decision of 17 December 1963, Yearbook vol 6, 1963, pp 278 et seq. Se also J. E. S. Fawcett, The Application of the European Convention on Human Rights, 1969, pp 48-52.

16. Op. cit. p 329. In a recent case, the Commission confirmed this opinion. Husmann Case, no 4653/73, Decision of 1 April 1974.

17. Decision of 1 February 1971, Yearbook vol 14, 1971, p 198, especially pp 220 et seq.

18. Reports in cases no 4464/70 para 69, and no 6514/72, para 71.

19. See, for example, Human Rights in National and International Law (Vienna Colloquy of 1965), Manchester 1968.

20. Eur. Court HR, Belgian Linguistic Cases, judgment of 23 July 1968, pp 34-35.

21. For a comparison of the decisions of national courts with those of the organs of the Convention, see the reports by T. Buergenthal and U. Scheuner, Vienna Colloquy of 1965, op. cit. pp 51 and 214.

22. Scheuner, op.cit. pp 248-9 and T. Opsahl in Privacy and Human Rights (Brussels Colloquy of 1970) pp 204-5.

23. M.-A. Eisen, Grenoble Colloquy 1973, HRJ vol VI, 1973, p 664.

24. Jean Raymond: Les droits garantis par la Convention de Sauvegarde des Droits de l'Homme, HRJ vol III, 1970, pp 289 et seq., especially p 292.

25. Eur. Court HR, Delcourt Case, judgment of 17 January 1970, p 19.
26. Eur. Court HR, Series B, Neumeister Case, pp 152 and 244.
27. Eur. Court HR, Neumeister Case, judgment of 27 June 1968.
28. Yearbook vol 6, 1963, pp 714 et seq.
29. Yearbook vol 14, 1971, p 476, and Stock-taking, DH (74) 6 pp 33-34.
30. Hermann Mosler: L'influence du droit national sur la Convention Européenne des Droits de l'Homme, in Miscellanea, W.J. Ganshof van der Meersch, 1972, vol I pp 521-43, especially p 533.
31. cf Frede Castberg: La Convention Européenne des Droits de l'Homme et l'idée de justice, in René Cassin, Amicorum Discipulorumque Liber, I pp 29 et seq.
32. Privacy and Human Rights, pp 182-253.
33. Frede Castberg: The European Convention on Human Rights, 1974, pp 83-85; J. E. S. Fawcett, op. cit. pp 34-41; Jean Raymond in HRJ vol III 1970, p 295; Stock-taking, DH (74) 6 pp 40-43.
34. Case no 5564/72, Decision of 14 December 1972, Collection of Decisions vol 42, p 114.
35. Case no 1802/62, Decision of 26 March 1963, Yearbook vol 6, 1963, p 481.
36. Case no 5961/72, Amekrane, Decision of 11 October 1973, Collection of Decisions vol 44, p 101, and Commission Report of 19 July 1974.
37. Yearbook vol 13, 1970, p 994.
38. See especially the report by Torkel Opsahl, Privacy and Human Rights pp 243-322, and the paper presented by W. Pahr: The meaning of the term "family" in the European Convention on Human Rights, in A. H. Robinson (ed) Privacy and Human Rights, Manchester, 1973, pp 275-83.
39. Castberg, op. cit. p 144.
40. Council of Europe, Consultative Assembly, Parliamentary Conference on Human Rights, Vienna 18-20 October 1971 (Strasbourg 1972).
41. See the Council of Europe publication: Convention for the Protection of Human Rights, Case-law topics, vol I "Human Rights in Prison" (1971), and vol 4 "Human Rights and their Limitations" (1974) pp 53-54.
42. Eur. Court HR, De Wilde, Ooms and Versyp Cases ("Vagrancy"), judgment of 18 June 1971 p 45.
43. Commission Report of 1 June 1973, para 97.
44. Judgment of 21 February 1975, para 37-40.
45. See in particular the decision of 8 March 1962 in the Isop Case, no 808/60, Yearbook vol 5, 1962, pp 108 et seq. (p 124), cf Marc-André Eissen: L'autonomie de l'article 14 de la Convention Européenne des Droits de l'Homme dans la jurisprudence de la Commission, Mélanges Modinos 1968, p 122-45.
46. Eur. Court HR, Belgian Linguistic Cases, judgment of 23 July 1968, p 33.

47. Ibid. p 34.
48. Yearbook vol 10, 1967, p 680.
49. Yearbook vol 6, 1963, p 732. In the Ofner and Hopfinger Cases, ibid p 696, the facts of the case led to a different conclusion.
50. Eur. Court HR, Neumeister Case, judgment of 27 June 1968, p 43.
51. Eur. Court HR, Golder Case, judgment of 21 February 1975, §§ 26-36.
52. See Jacques Velu in Revue de Droit international et de Droit comparé, 1961, pp 140-60; Christian Rasenack: "Civil Rights and Obligations" or "Droits et obligations de caractère civil" ... HRJ vol III, 1970, pp 51-81.
53. See Jean Raymond in HRJ vol III, 1970, pp 301-02.
54. See majority opinion of the Commission, Report of 19 March 1970, Eur. Court HR, Series B vol 11, Ringeisen Case, pp 71-72.
55. Eur. Court HR, Ringeisen Case, judgment of 16 July 1971, p 39.
56. Eur. Court HR, Series B vol 11, Ringeisen Case, p 241, Hearing of 9 March 1971.
57. Ibid pp 243-44.
58. Judgment pp 39-40.
59. René Cassin: De la place faite aux devoirs de l'individu dans la Déclaration universelle des Droits de l'Homme, in Mélanges Modinos 1968, pp 479-88.
60. M.-A. Eissen: La Convention et les devoirs de l'individu, in La Protection internationale des Droits de l'Homme, Colloquy 14-15 November 1960, pp 167-94, and Une mise à jour, in René Cassin, Amicorum Discipulorum-que Liber III, pp 151-62, and several other contributions to the same volume; Andreas Khol, Zwischen Staat und Weltstaat, Vienna, 1969, pp 309-18; Castberg op.cit. pp 12-13.
61. Case no 2646/65, Decision of 30 March 1966, Yearbook vol 9, 1966, p 490.
62. Case no 4125/69, Decision of 1 February 1971, Yearbook vol 14, 1971, p 198.
63. Cases no 4464/70, Belgian National Police Union, and no 5614/72, Svenska Lokmannaförbundet.
64. Case no 4464/70, Commission Report § 59, and no 5614/72, Report § 62.

Bibliografi

over professor dr. jur. Max Sørensens værker

Bibliography

of the works of professor, dr. jur. Max Sørensen

Indledning

Nedenstående fortegnelse over Max Sørensens offentliggjorte værker er i overensstemmelse med traditionen opstillet kronologisk med fortløbende nummerering af de enkelte titler.

Indenfor det enkelte år er følgende rækkefølge anvendt: bøger, tidsskriftartikler, anmeldelser af andre forfatteres værker og aviskronikker.

Nye udgaver af bøger er anført under den nyeste udgaves udgivelsesår med krydshenvisning.

Andre forfatteres anmeldelser af Max Sørensens værker er anført i alfabetisk orden under det anmeldte værk.

Titlen på det tidsskrift, festsskrift m.v., hvori afhandlinger og andre værker er optaget, er trykt med kursiv.

Som sagkyndig i folkeret for Udenrigsministeriet har Max Sørensen udarbejdet et betydeligt antal responsa, der kun undtagelsesvis er offentliggjort.

Op mod halvdelen af værkerne er på fremmede sprog. Bidrag til publikationer fra internationale organisationer er kun angivet på ét af organisationens officielle sprog.

Der er kun anvendt en enkelt tidsskriftforkortelse, UfR: Ugeskrift for Retsvæsen. Efter bibliografiens kronologiske del, A, følger en summarisk systematisk del, B, ordnet efter emneområder med henvisning til de ved de enkelte titler anførte numre.

Introduction

For the benefit of foreign readers the introduction to the bibliography is in English as well as in Danish.

The following list of the published works of Max Sørensen is according to tradition chronological with consecutive numbering of the titles.

Titles published within a year are grouped as follows: books, articles, reviews by Max Sørensen and last newspaper articles.

Later editions of books are listed under the year of publication of the later edition with cross reference.

Reviews by other authors of Max Sørensen's books are listed in alphabetic order below the title reviewed.

The title of the periodical, book or newspaper, containing an article by Max Sørensen, is printed in italics.

The list only contains published works. As specialist in public international law for the Ministry of Foreign Affairs, Max Sørensen has prepared a number of expert opinions, which are not published except in very few cases.

Almost half of the works are in languages other than Danish. Contributions to publications of international organizations have only been listed in one of the official languages of the organization.

The title of only one periodical is abbreviated. *UfR:* Ugeskrift for Retsvæsen.

After the chronological part, A, follows a summary systematic part, B, grouped according to subject with reference to the numbers given to individual titles in part A.

A. Kronologisk del
Chronological Section

1932

1. Hævd og Forældelse i Folkeretten. *Nordisk Tidsskrift for international Ret* 3. 1932 p 239-262.
2. La prescription en droit international. *Acta Scandinavica Juris Gentium* 1932 p 145-170.
3. Om Justitieombudsmanden. *Juristen* 1932 p 65-68 Cf No 52.

1934

4. Betingelserne for Traktaters Afslutning efter Folkeretten og efter Danmarks og de vigtigste fremmede Landes Forfatninger. 1935 307 s + 50 s. noter. (Besvarelse af Københavns Universitets Prisopgave 1934. Retsvidenskab A. Guldmedaille 1935, jfr Københavns Universitets Aarsskrift 1935 p 164-165. Dupliceret i få eksemplarer).
5. Traktatsamling til Studie- og Eksamensbrug. Ved Christian Eggert, Lauge R. Kallestrup og Max Sørensen. Gad København 1934 43 s (2. udg. ved Tyge Heilesen og Kjeld Lundgren 1938. 59 s).

1936

6. Om Juristens praktiske Uddannelse. *Juristen* 1936, p 125-131.
7. Juristernes økonomiske Forhold i Studietiden. *Juristen 1936 p 196-200.*
8. Et Spørgsmål vedrørende uskiftet Bo. *Fuldmægtigen* 1936 p 67-70.

1937

9. Professor Axel Møller in memoriam. *Stud.jur.* 1937/38 nr. 4 p 3.

1938

10. Versailles-Traktatens Slesvigske Bestemmelser og Suverænitetens Overdragelse. *Håndbog i det Slesvigske Spørgsmåls Historie*, Bd. 2 1938 p 541-557.
11. The modification of collective treaties without the consent of

all the contracting parties. *Acta Scandinavica Juris gentium 9:* 1938
p 150-173.
12. Om kollektive Traktaters Ændring uden Samtykke af alle kon-
traherende Parter. *Nordisk Tidsskrift for international Ret* 9: 1938
p 343-366.
13. Artikler i Den lille Salmonsen Bd. 4-6 Schultz 1938-39
(Bogstav F-I)
Falskmønterikonventionen. Bd 4 1938 p 64.
Fiskeritraktater. Bd 4 1938 p 204-205.
Flaadetraktater. Bd 4 1938 p 217.
Flygtninge. Bd 4 1938 p 247-248.
Folkenes Forbund Bd 4 1938 p 285-287.
Folkeret. Bd 4 1938 p 287-288.
Folkeretlige Servitutter. Bd 4 1938 p 288-289.
Forligsnævn. Bd 4 1938 p 336.
Forsvarsforbund. Bd 4 1938 p 356-357.
Fredsbrud. Bd 4 1938 p 459.
Fredsslutning. Bd 4 1938 p 459-460.
Generalakten. Bd 4 1938 p 669.
Genève-Konventionen. Bd 4 1938 p 675.
Genève-Protokollen. Bd 4 1938 p 675.
Gesandt. Bd 4 1938 p 703-704.
Gesandtskab. Bd 4 1938 p 704.
Grænse. Bd 5 1938 p 158-159.
Haag-Domstol. Bd 5 1938 p 255.
Haag-Konferencerne. Bd 5 1938 p 255-256.
Haag-Reglerne. Bd 5 1938 p 256.
Handelstraktater. Bd 5 1938 p 335-336.
Hav. Bd 5 1938 p 391-392.
Ikke-Indblanding. Bd 6 1939 p 80-81.
Integritet. Bd 6 1939 p 165-166.
Internationale domstole. Bd 6 1939 p 173.
Internationale unioner. Bd 6 1939 p 174.
International privatret. Bd 6 1939 p 175.
Internering. Bd 6 1939 p 175.
Intervention. Bd 6 1939 p 177.

1939

14. Max Sørensen et Erik Bondo Svane: Les conventions contractées entre le Danemark et l'Allemagne du fait de la réunion du Slesvig du Nord avec le Danemark. *Manuel historique de la question du Slesvig 1906-1938*, Reitzel, Copenhague et Pédone, Paris 1939 p 628-634.

1942

15. Anmeldelse af Erik Brüel: Internationale Stræder. En folkeretlig undersøgelse. 1939-40. *UfR* 1942 B 11-16.

1946

16. Les Sources du Droit International. Étude sur la Jurisprudence de la Cour Permanente de Justice Internationale. Munksgaard, Copenhague 1946. 274 p. (Thèse du doctorat).
    Reviews in alphabetic order:
    Boeg, N. V. *Nordisk Tidsskrift for international Ret* 18: 1947/48 p 68-70.
    Finch, G. A. *American journal of international law* 41: 1947 p 703-704.
    Gonicéc, P. F. *Revue générale de droit international public* 1948 p 281.
    Hambro, Edv. *Tidsskrift for Rettsvitenskap* 1946 p 569-572.
    J., M. J. *British yearbook of international law* 24: 1947 p 515-516.
    Martin, A. *International law quarterly* 1947 p 255-257.
    Ross, Alf *UfR* 1947 B 161-170.
    Sachs, P. M. *Juristen* 1948 p 341-348.

1948

17. Palæstina. *Randers Amtsavis* 16. april 1948.

1949

18. Bemærkninger om Det såkaldte Funktionelle Princip i International Organisation. *Jus Gentium. Nordisk Tidsskrift for Folkeret og international Privatret* 1949 p 83-104. (With a summary in English p 104-106).

19. Menneskerettighederne og Mindretalsbeskyttelse. *Jus Gentium* 1949 p 184-189.

20. Det europæiske Råd. Hovedtræk af dets tilblivelse og forfatning. *Jus Gentium* 1949 p 209-237.

21. Domicil og Eksterritorialitet. *Jus Gentium* 1949 p 392-395 (ad UfR 1948. 1120H).
22. Den danske Grundlovs regler om parlamentarisk kontrol med udenrigspolitiken. *Tidsskrift for Rettsvitenskap* 1949 p 97-140.
23. De Forenede Nationers rolle i verdenspolitiken. *Gads danske Magasin* 1949 p 559-575.
24. Review. Lazare Kopelmanas: L'organisation des Nations Unies. I. L'organisation constitutionelle des NU. 1. Les Sources constitutionelles de L'ONU. Paris 1947. *Jus Gentium* 1949 p 200-203.
25. Review. H. T. Adam: L'organisation européenne de coopération économique. Paris 1949. *Jus Gentium* 1949 p 323-324.
26. Review. Fritz Grob: The relativity of war and peace. New Haven 1949. *Jus Gentium* 1949 p 398-399.
27. Review. Current legal problems 1-2. 1948-1949. London. *Jus Gentium* 1949 p 399.
28. Notes on human rights in Denmark. *Yearbook on Human Rights*. For 1947. United Nations, New York 1949 p 86-87.
29. Rio-Traktaten. Atlanterhavspagtens Forbillede? *Berlingske Tidende* 2.1.1949.
30. Det Britiske Rige og Vesteuropa. *Randers Amtsavis* 19.1.1949.

1950
31. Kan domstolene efterprøve forvaltningens skønsmæssige afgørelser? *UfR* 1950 p 273-295. (Foredrag).
32. Notes on human rights in Denmark. *Yearbook on Human Rights*. For 1948. United Nations, New York 1950 p 55-57.
33. Menneskerettighederne. *Den jydske Akademiker* 23: 1950/51 nr. 1 p 6-9.
34. Danmarks Søterritorium. *Jus Gentium* 2: 1950 p 181-199. (Forelæsning holdt ved Lunds Universitet d. 16. oktober 1950).
35. Review in English of: Alf Ross: Constitution of the United Nations. Analysis of function and structure. Copenhagen 1950. *Jus Gentium* 2: 1950 p 245-249.
36. Review. Georg Schwarzenberger: International law. 1. International law as applied by international courts and tribunals. London 1949. *The Solicitor,* London 17: 1950 p 70-71.

37. Om anerkendelse af nye regeringer. *Berlingske Aftenavis* 27. marts 1950.
38. Adgangen til Østersøen. *Politiken* 23. juni 1950.
39. Dansk suverænitet og Atlantenhedskommando. *Politiken* 21. september 1950.

1951

40. Nyere udviklingslinier i international organisation. *Statsvetenskaplig Tidsskrift* 1951 p 113-129.
41. FN behandler menneskerettighederne. Forord af Max Sørensen. Udarb. af FN-gruppen ved Aarhus Universitet 1951. 47s.
42. Notes on human rights in Denmark. *Yearbook on Human Rights.* For 1949. United Nations, New York 1951 p 57.
43. FN's arbejde for mellemfolkelig ret og sikkerhed. *Freds-Bladet* 60: 1951 p 97-100.
44. Kronik i Politiken 28.3.1951 i anledning af Alf Ross: To Verdener. *Politiken* 21.3.1951.
45. Administration og retssikkerhed. *Politiken* 14.8.1951 (Kronik).

1952

46. Grundtræk af International Organisation. Munksgaard. København 1952. 184 s.
    Anmeldelser/reviews.
    Fischer, Paul *Juristen* 1953 p 91-94.
    Hambro, Edv. *Nordisk Tidsskrift for International Ret* 1953 p 55.
    Torkild-Hansen, Carl *Sagførerbladet* 1952 p 178.
47. Le Conseil de l'Europe. *Académie de Droit International. Receueil des Cours.* Tome 81 1952 p 121-198.
48. The Council of Europe. A new experiment in international organization. *The Year Book of World Affairs,* London 6: 1952 p 75-97.
49. La juridiction criminelle internationale dans un système de sécurité collective. *Politique Etrangère,* 1952 p 113-126.
50. Federal States and the International Protection of Human Rights. *American Journal of International Law, Washington* 46: 1952 p 195-218.
51. Replik om domstolsprøvelse af forvaltningens skøn. *UfR* 1952 B 289-294. Jfr. Poul Andersen B 225-232.

52. Om justitieombudsmanden. *Juristen* 1952 p 65-68. Cf. No 3.
53. Menneskerettighedernes historie. *Tidsskrift for Dansk Røde Kors* 1952 p 171-174.
54. Användningen av fri prövning inom förvaltningen. *Nordisk administrativt Tidsskrift* 1952 p 290-295. (Diskussionsindlæg på Det nordiske administrative Forbunds 10. almindelige møde i Helsingfors 1952).
55. Et fremskridt. Om forslagene til pas og fremmedlovgivning. *UfR* 1952 B 101-105.
56. Problèmes politiques contemporains du Danemark. *Revue Française de Science Politique*, Paris 1952 p 737-751.
57. Notes on human rights in Denmark. *Yearbook on Human Rights*. For 1950. United Nations, New York 1952 p 67-68.
58. Review. Georg Schwarzenberger: Power politics. A study of international society. London 1951. *The year book of world affairs* 6: 1952 p 276-278.
59. Review. L. C. Green: International law through the cases. London 1951. *The year book of world affairs* 6: 1952 p 856-857.
60. Svar på manges bekymringer. Er der efter planerne om Tysklands genoprustning grund til at revidere vor tilslutning til Atlantpagten? *Politiken* 25.10.1952. (Kronik).

1953

61. Le statut juridique du Groënland. *Revue juridique et politique de l'Union Française*. Paris 7: 1953 p 425-442.
62. Responsum vedrørende de problemer, der knytter sig til Grundlovens § 18. *Betænkning afgivet af Forfatningskommissionen af 1946*, 1953 p 113-127.
63. Debatten om revision af De Forenede Nationers Pagt. *Økonomi og Politik* 27: 1953 p 307-317.
64. Notes on human rights in Denmark. *Yearbook on Human Rights*. For 1951. United Nations, New York 1953 p 68.
65. Anm. af Frede Castberg: Studier i Folkerett. Oslo 1952. *Tidsskrift for Rettsvitenskap* 1953 p 90-95.
66. Den omstridte paragraf 20 i den nye grundlov. *Politiken* 17. maj 1953.

1954

67. The draft statute of an international criminal court. *International Bar Association. Fourth international conference, Madrid 1952.* The Hague 1954 p 71-79.
68. Notes on human rights in Denmark. *Yearbook on Human Rights.* For 1952. United Nations, New York 1954 p 47-48.
69. Anm. af Hilding Eek: Freedom of Information as a Project of International Legislation. Uppsala 1953. *Statsvetenskaplig Tidsskrift* 57: 1954 p 100-103.

1955

70. Bør F.N.'s Pagt ændres? Forlaget Fremad, København 1955 47 s. Cf No 63.
71. Le Conseil Nordique. *Revue générale de Droit international Public* 58: 1955 p 63-84.
72. Notes on human rights in Denmark. *Yearbook on Human Rights.* For 1953. United Nations, New York 1955 p 62-67.
73. Anm. af N. Møllmann og S. A. Hjermov: *Håndbog for danske kommuner.* 1954-55. *UfR* 1955 B 286-288.

1956

74. Denmark and The United Nations. By Max Sørensen and Niels J. Haagerup. Manhattan Publishing Company, New York 1956. 167 p. (National Studies on International Organization).
   Reviews in alphabetic order:
   Potter, P. B. *American journal of international law* 51: 1957 p 447.
   Seidl-Hohenveldern, I. *American journal of comparative law* 7: 1958 p 109.
75. The Quest for Equality. *International Conciliation*, No 507, New York, 1956 p 290-346.
76. Konstitusjonelle spørsmål som oppstår ved statens deltagelse i internasjonale organisasjoner. *Forhandlinger på det 20. nordiske juristmøte i Oslo 1954.* Oslo 1956 p 66-69 (Korreferent).
77. Gesandt, dr.jur. Georg Cohn. *Nordisk Tidsskrift for international Ret* 26: 1956 p 80-81 (Nekrolog).

1957

78. Notes on human rights in Denmark. *Yearbook on Human Rights.* For 1954. United Nations, New York 1957 p 76-77.

79. Anm. af Poul Meyer: Administrative Organization. A Comparative Study of the Organization of Public Administration. London-København 1957. *UfR* 1957 B 137-140.

80. Anm. af Paul Henning Fischer: Det europæiske Kul- og Stålfællesskab. 1957. *Juristen* 1957 p 486-493.

81. FN og fremtiden. *Politiken* 1. januar 1957 (Kronik).

82. Suverænitetsbegrebet under omdannelse. *Aarhus Stiftstidende* 11. og 12. september 1957. (Tale ved Aarhus Universitets Årsfest 11. september 1957).

83. The Law of the Sea. *International Conciliation* No 520. Carnegie Endowment for International Peace, New York 1958/59 p 193-256.

84. Internationale forvaltningsoverenskomster. (Summary in English p 47). *Nordisk administrativt Tidsskrift* 1958 p 28-47.

85. Om retten til diplomatisk beskyttelse. *Festskrift til professor Poul Andersen* 1958 p 398-412.

86. Poul Andersen 1888 - 12. juni – 1958. *Festskrift til professor Poul Andersen* 1958 p 1-6.

87. Genève-konferencen 1958 om havets retsorden. *Nordisk Tidsskrift for international Ret* 28: 1958 p 86-93 (Foredrag).

88. Bør studietiden ved de højere læreanstalter afkortes? Og hvorledes kan det gøres? En enquête blandt professorer, administrationschefer og akademiske organisationsledere. *Samraadet* 1958 p 95-106, 111-115. (Indlæg af bl.a. Max Sørensen).

89. Notes on human rights in Denmark. *Yearbook on Human Rights.* For 1955. United Nations, New York 1958 p 45-46.

90. Hvordan vil Det europæiske Fællesmarked begrænse vor suverænitet? *Dansk Toldtidende* 56: 1958 p 92-97 (Radioforedrag).

1959

91. The territorial sea of archipelagos. *Varia Juris Gentium. Liber Amicorum, aangeboden aan Jean Pierre Adrien François. Nederlands Tijdschrift voor Internationnaal Recht,* Leiden 1959 p 315-331 (Special issue).

92. Om loves bekendtgørelse og ikrafttræden. *UfR* 1959 B 112-116 og B 10-11. Jfr Alf Ross B 24-30 om tøbrudsdommen.
93. Notes on human rights in Denmark. *Yearbook on Human Rights.* For 1956. United Nations, New York 1959 p 50.
94. Anm. af Bent Christensen: Nævn og råd. 1958. *Nordisk administrativt Tidsskrift* 1959 p 86-92.
95. Et nyt forfatningsretligt værk. Anm. af Alf Ross: Dansk Statsforfatningsret I 1959 og Statsretlige Studier 1959. *Juristen* 1959 p 441-457.

1960
96. Principes de Droit International Public. Cours Général. *Académie de Droit International. Recueil des Cours.* Tome 101. Leyden 1960 p 1-254.
97. The International Court of Justice: its role in contemporary international relations. *International Organization* 14: 1960 p 261-276. Cf No 128.
98. Review of: The British Yearbook of International Law 1958. Oxford 1959. *International Affairs* 36: 1960 p 94-95.

1961
99. Dansk folkeretlig praksis i 1960. *Nordisk Tidsskrift for international Ret* 31: 1961 p 124-132.
100. Notes on human rights in Denmark. *Yearbook on Human Rights.* For 1959. United Nations, New York 1961 p 85-86.
101. Anm. af Isi Foighel: Nationalisering af fremmed ejendom. 1961. *Juristen* 1961 p 543-548.
102. Review of: The British Yearbook of International Law 1959. Oxford 1960. *International Affairs* 37: 1961 p 361-362.

1962
103. Afgiver vi vor selvstændighed? *Danmark og De Seks.* Fremtiden 1962 14-21.
104. Danmarks selvstændighed og Det europæiske Fællesmarked. *Fremtiden* 17: 1962 nr 2 p 11-15. (Optrykt i Dansk Europaunions Europa-Kronik nr. 1, 1962).
105. Udtalelse til belysning af administrationens beføjelser overfor den lovgivende forsamling til at afholde ubevilgede udgifter. *Folketingstidende 1962-1963. Tillæg B* sp. 1021-1066.

106. Notes on human rights in Denmark. *Yearbook on Human Rights.* For 1960. United Nations, New York 1962 p 93.
107. Review of: The British Yearbook of International Law 1960. Oxford 1961. *International Affairs* 38: 1962 p 395-396.
108. Grundloven og Rom-Traktaten. *Information* 10. april 1962 og 1. maj 1962. (Diskussion med Harald Høgsbro).
109. Internationale Organisationer i Vesteuropa. Akademisk Boghandel, Århus 1963, med enkelte rettelser og tilføjelser 1965. 145 bl. (Duplikeret).
110. Pirate broadcasting from the High Seas. *Legal essays. A tribute to Frede Castberg.* Universitetsforlaget, Oslo 1963 p 319-331.
111. Det europæiske økonomiske Fællesskab og Danmarks Grundlov. *Juristen* 1963 p 57-85.
112. Den akademiske frihed. *Stud.jur.* 1963 p 131-133.
113. Kort bemærkning om loves ikrafttræden. *UfR* 1963 B 10-11.
114. Notes on human rights in Denmark. *Yearbook on Human Rights.* For 1961. United Nations, New York 1963 p 91-97.
115. Review. The British Yearbook of International Law 1961. Oxford 1962. *International Affairs* 39: 1963 p 573-574.

1964

116. Retlige problemer vedrørende uforudsete udgifter i det financielle bevillingssystem. *Nordisk administrativt Tidsskrift* 1964 p 273-293, 315-317. (Foredrag ved Det Nordiske administrative Forbunds 14. almindelige møde i Oslo 1964 med efterfølgende diskussion, ibid p 293-317).
117. Bemærkninger om traktatbestemmelsers gennemførelse i dansk ret. *Juristen* 1964 p 253-256.
118. Notes on human rights in Denmark. *Yearbook on Human Rights.* For 1962. United Nations, New York 1964 p 70.
119. Anm. af Morris Davis: Iceland extends its fisheries limits. Oslo 1963. *Juristen* 1964 p 199.

1965

120. Völkerrechtlicher Schutz der Menschenrechte. *Fünfzig Jahre Institut für Internationales Recht an der Universität Kiel.* Hansischer Gildenverlag. Hamburg 1965 p 22-33.
121. Review of: The British Yearbook of International Law 1962. Oxford 1964. *International Affairs* 41: 1965 p 102-103.

1966

122. Finansloven. Noter til Statsforfatningsretten. Akademisk Forlag 1966. 33 s. (Multigraferet).
123. Spørgsmålet om den umiddelbare anvendelse af traktater som bestanddel af dansk ret. *Nordisk administrativt Tidsskrift* 1966 p 107-123. (Summary in English p 123-124).
124. Notes on human rights in Denmark. *Yearbook on Human Rights.* For 1964. United Nations, New York 1966 p 98.
125. Review of: The British Yearbook of International Law 1963. Oxford 1965. *International Affairs* 42:1966 p 111-113.

1967

126. Den internationale beskyttelse af menneskerettighederne. Munksgaard 1967. 87 s. (Søndagsuniversitetet 82)
Anmeldelser:
Castberg, Frede *Lov og Rett* 1967 p 378-379.
Petrén, Sture *Juristen* p 181-185.
127. Die Verpflichtungen eines Staates im Bereich seiner nationalen Rechtsordnung auf Grund eines Staatsvertrages. Bericht. *Menschenrechte im Staatsrecht und im Völkerrecht. Vorträge und Diskussionen des Zweiten Internationalen Kolloquiums über die Europäische Konvention zum Schutze der Menschenrechte und Grundfreiheiten.* Verlag C. F. Müller, Karlsruhe 1967 p 15-33 (Cf No 133, 134).
128. The International Court of Justice. *The United Nations. International organization and administration.* Ed. by Maurice Waters. London/New York 1967 p 122-132. Cf No 97.
129. Review of: The British Yearbook of International Law 1964. Oxford 1966. *International Affairs* 43: 1967 p 113-114.

1968

130. Editor-in-chief of: Manual of Public International Law. Carnegie Endowment for International Peace, Macmillan, London 1968, 930 p. Spanish edition 1973.
Reviews in alphabetic order:
Brownlie, I. *British yearbook of international law* 42: 1969 p 352-356.
Fleischer, C. A. *Tidsskrift for Rettsvitenskap* 1968 p 642-649.
Hambro, Edv. *Nordisk Tidsskrift for international Ret* 39: 1969 p 61-65.

Johnson, D. H. N. *Law quarterly review* 1969 p 120-124.

Lissitzyn, O. J. *Columbia law review* 68: 1968 p 1623-1625.

Opsahl, T. *Svensk Juristtidning* 1971 p 745.

Stone, J. *American journal of international law* 1969 p 157.

131. Institutionalized international co-operation in economic, social and cultural fields. *Manual of Public International Law*, Macmillan, London 1968 p 605-671.

132. Plaidoirie dans l'Affaire linguistique. *Publications de la Cour Européenne des Droits de l'Homme*. Série B. Strasbourg. Vol. 1 1967 p 514-522, 527-528. Vol. 2 1968 p 176-179.

133. Obligations of a state party to a treaty, as regards its municipal law. *Human Rights in National and International Law*, Manchester 1968 p 11-31. (The Proceedings of the Second International Conference on the European Convention on Human Rights held in Vienna) (Cf No 127, 134).

134. Obligations d'un Etat partie à un traité sur le plan de son droit interne. *Les droits de l'homme en droit interne et en droit international*. Presses Universitaires de Bruxelles 1968 p 38-61. (Actes du 2e colloque international sur la Convention Européenne des Droits de l'Homme, Vienne, 18-20 octobre 1965) (Cf No 127, 133).

135. Séance spéciale de l'Assemblée Consultative du Conseil de l'Europe pour la celébration de l'Année Internationale des Droits de l'Homme. Conseil de l'Europe 1968 p 31-35.

136. Le problème inter-temporel dans l'application de la Convention Européenne des Droits de l'Homme. *Mélanges offerts à Polys Modinos. Problèmes des droits de l'homme et de l'unification européenne.* Pédone, Paris 1968 p 304-319.

137. Aktuelle problemer vedrørende den internationale beskyttelse af menneskerettighederne. *Christiansborg-Seminariet om menneskerettighederne.* Dansk Samråd for Forenede Nationer 1968 p 8-13.

1969

138. Statsforfatningsret. Juristforbundets Forlag, København 1969. 432 s. Jfr. nr. 163/170.
Anmeldelse
Lorenzen, Peer *Juristen* 1972 p 420-432.

139. Kompendium i Folkeret. Akademisk Boghandel ved Aarhus Universitet 1969. 47 s. (Duplikeret).

140. Dissenting opinion in *International Court of Justice. Reports of judgments, advisory opinions and orders. North Sea Continental Shelf Cases. (Federal Republic of Germany/Denmark: Federal Republic of Germany/Netherlands). Judgment of 20. February 1969.* The Hague 1969 p 242-258. (Title and text in English and French).

141. Plaidoirie dans l'Affaire »Wemhoff«. *Publications de la Cour Européenne des Droits de l'Homme.* Série B vol. 5, p 258-275, 288-294. Strasbourg 1969.

142. Plaidoirie dans l'Affaire »Neumeister«. *Publications de la Cour Européenne des Droits de l'Homme.* Série B vol. 6, p 197-219. Strasbourg 1969.

143. La recevabilité de l'instance devant la Cour Européenne des Droits de l'Homme. Notes sur les rapports entre la Commission et la Cour. *René Cassin. Amicorum Discipulorumque Liber I: Problèmes de protection internationale des droits de l'homme.* Pédone, Paris 1969 p 333-346.

144. Til Alf Ross på 70 års dagen. *UfR* 1969 B 210-211. (Tale ved overrækkelsen af festskriftet).

145. Review of: The British Yearbook of International Law 1965-66. Oxford 1968. *International Affairs:* 45: 1969 p 118-119.

1970

146. Responsum om regeringens afgørelse i »Laksesagen«. *Dansk Fiskeritidende* 88: 1970 nr. 48 p 6-7. Jfr. G. L. Mourier p 7-8 (Laksefiskeri udfor Nordnorge).

147. Plaidoirie dans l'Affaire »Delcourt«. *Publications de la Cour Européenne des Droits de l'Homme.* Série B p 157-165 et p 235-240. Strasbourg 1970.

148. FN's mulighed som fredsbevarende organ med særligt henblik på Danmarks sikkerhed. Problemer omkring Danmarks sikkerhedspolitik. *Fremtiden* 1970 p 199-213.

149. Die Griechenlandfrage – eine verlorene Chance. *Oesterreichische Zeitschrift für Aussenpolitik* 1970 p 43-46.

150. Torben Lund. 12. oktober 1902-25. januar 1970. *Aarsberetning for Aarhus Universitet* 1969-1970 p 17-19. (In memoriam).

151. Review of: The British Yearbook of International Law 1967. Oxford 1969. *International Affairs* 46: 1970 p 113-114.
152. Forpasset mulighed. Da menneskerettighederne blev ofret. *Politiken* 5. januar 1970. (Kronik).
153. Folkeret. Nogle hovedproblemer i det internationale retssystem. Berlingske Forlag 1971. 167 s. (Berlingske Leksikon Bibliotek. Jura 55).
Anmeldelse
Espersen, Ole *Politiken* 20.9.1971.
Thylstrup, Asger *Berlingske Tidende* 28.12.1971.
154. Plaidoirie dans l'Affaire »De Wilde, Ooms et Versyp«. *Publications de la Cour Européenne des Droits de l'Homme* Série B vol. 10, p 257-263, 271-272, 274-279, 290-301, 307-309, 316-317, 357-367, 370-373, 383-384. Strasbourg 1971 (Cf No 172).
155. Forfatningsretlige problemer i forbindelse med Danmarks indtræden i De Europæiske Fællesskaber. *Juristen* 1971 p 434-440. (Udtalelse til Folketingets markedsudvalg).
156. Ombudsmanden og europæisk integration. *Festskrift til Stephan Hurwitz* 1971 p 499-515.
157. En berigtigelse *UfR* 1971 B 17. Jfr Knud Illum UfR 1970 B 245-256 om domsbegrundelse.
158. Grundloven og dansk medlemsskab i Europa-fællesskabet *Fremtiden* 26: 1971 nr. 5 p 27-33 (Udtalelse til Folketingets markedsudvalg).
159. Anm. af Ole Espersen: Indgåelse og Opfyldelse af Traktater. 1970. *Juristen* 1971 p 144-148.
160. Anm. af Frede Castberg: Den europæiske konvensjon om menneskerettighetene. Oslo 1971. *Tidsskrift for Rettsvitenskap* 1971 p 663-670.
161. Danmarks Grundlov og Rom-Traktaten. *Weekendavisen Berlingske Aften*, 12-13. februar 1971.
162. Vort fælles hav. *Politiken* 22. april 1971. (Kommentar).

1972
163. Tillæg til Statsforfatningsret 1969. Kap. 15 A. Forfatningsretlige problemer som følge af dansk medlemskab af De europæiske Fællesskaber. 1972. 17 s. Jfr nr. 138, 170.
164. EFs institutioner. Råd, Kommission og Parlament i et samspil

under Domstolens legalitetskontrol. *Fremtiden* 27: 1972 nr. 4 p 21-28.

165. EF og Grundloven – endnu engang. *Juristen* 1972 p 117-129. Jfr Erik Siesby 1971 p 414-434.

166. Die Anwendung des Rechts der Europäischen Gemeinschaften in Dänemark. – *Die Erweiterung der Europäischen Gemeinschaften.* Heymann. Köln 1972 p 1-23, s. auch Gert Nicolaysen p 109-112 (Kölner Schriften zum Europarecht Bd. 15).

167. Compétences supranationales et pouvoirs constitutionnels en droit danois. *Miscellanea W. J. Ganshof van der Meersch* 2, 1972 p 481-492.

168. Om tågeslør og en enkel og klar sandhed. Det folkeretlige grundlag er i orden. *Politiken* 9. juni 1972. (Debatten om Grundloven og EF).

169. Historie og logik i EF-diskussionen. Stem ja eller nej, men det er ikke lovbrud at gå med. *Politiken* 12. juni 1972.

1973

170. Statsforfatningsret. 2. udg. ved Peter Germer. *Juristforbundets Forlag* 1973. 454 s. 6. oplag 1987. Jfr nr. 138, 163.

171. Le problème dit du droit intertemporel dans l'ordre international. Rapport. *Annuaire de l'Institut de Droit International* 55: 1973 p 1-66. Rapport définitif ibid p 85-98. (Cf No 179).

172. Plaidoirie dans l'Affaire »de Wilde, Ooms et Versyp« (art. 50). *Publications de la Cour Européenne des Droits de l'Homme* Série B, vol. 12 p 45-52. Strasbourg 1973 (Cf No 154).

173. Danske domstoles anvendelse af EF's regler. *Juristen* 1973 p 1-17. (Foredrag holdt på Den danske Dommerforenings årsmøde 1972. Særlig om EF-Traktatens art. 177).

174. The Enlargement of the European Communities and the Protection of Human Rights. *European Yearbook* for 1971 19: 1973 p 3-17. (Résumé en français p 17-22).

175. Anm. af Peter Germer: Ytringsfrihedens væsen. 1973. *Juristen* 1973 p 358-361.

176. Denmark and the United Nations. By Max Sørensen and Niels J. Haagerup. Greenwood Press, Westport, Conn. 1974. 154 p.

177. Domstolene i Danmark. *Domstolarnas roll i samhället. Seminarium* 1972. Rättsfonden 1974 p 62-70.

178. Den nationella suveräniteten. *Vår Lösen. Ekumenisk Kulturtids-skrift*, Sigtuna 65: 1974 p 325-329.

1975

179. Le problème dit du droit intertemporel dans l'ordre international. *Annuaire de l'Institut de Droit International* 56: 1975 p 339-374 (Cf No 171).
180. L'expérience d'un membre de la Commission Européenne des Droits de l'Homme. *Revue des Droits de l'Homme* 7: 1975 p 329-342.
181. I diritti iscritti della Convenzione dei Diritti dell'unomo nel 1950 hanno lo stesso significato nel 1975? *Rivista di diritto europeo*, Roma 15: 1975 p 267-300 (Cf No 183, 189).
182. Brückenbau und Durchfahrten in Meerengen. *Recht im Dienst des Friedens. Festschrift für Eberhard Menzel*. Duncker und Humblot, Berlin 1975 p 551-563.

1976

183. Les droits inscrits en 1950 dans la Convention Européenne des Droits de l'Homme ont-ils la même signification en 1975? *Actes du quatrième colloque international sur la Convention Européenne des Droits de l'Homme, Rome 5-8 novembre 1975*. Conseil de l'Europe, Strasbourg 1976 p 85-110. (Also with title and text in English: Proceedings. Also in *Jus Gentium* 10: 1978 p 59-108, cf No 189).

1977

184. Berührungspunkte zwischen der Europäischen Menschenrechtskonvention und dem Recht der Europäischen Gemeinschaften. *Mitteilungen über den Gerichtshof der Europäischen Gemeinschaften*. Luxembourg 1977 Heft 3 p 41-52 (In the languages of the official publications of the Court) (Cf No 186).
185. Sture Petrén. In memoriam. *Nordisk Tidsskrift for international Ret* 1977 p 3-6.

1978

186. Berührungspunkte zwischen der Europäischen Menschenrechtskonvention und dem Recht der Europäischen Gemein-

schaften. *Europäische Grundrechte. Zeitschrift* 5: 1978 p 33-36 (Cf No 184).

187. Punti di contatto tra la convenzione europea dei diritti dell'uomo ed il diritto delle Communità europee. *Rivista di diritto europeo.* Roma 18: 1978 p 163-172. (Cf No 184, 186).

188. Den europæiske Menneskerettighedskonventions placering i folkeretten. *Menneskerettigheder i Vesteuropa. Artikelsamling.* 1978 p 20-23. (Cf No 190).

189. Les droits inscrits en 1950 dans la Convention européenne des droits de l'homme ont-ils la même signification en 1975? *Jus Gentium.* Roma 10: 1978 p 59-108. (Cf No 183).

190. Den europæiske Menneskerettighedskonventions placering i folkeretten. *Vestkysten* 2. september 1978. (Cf No 188).

1979

191. Teheran og folkeretten. *Jyllands-Posten* 4.12.1979 (Ambassadebesættelsen og gidseltagningen).

1980

192. Et spørgsmål om begrundelse af forvaltningsakter – i EF-retligt perspektiv. *UfR* 1980 B 349-353. (Kommentar til dommen i UfR 1980. 504 H om udvisning af franskmand).

193. Review in German. Kari Joutsamo: The role of preliminary rulings in the European Communities. Helsinki 1979. *Zeitschrift für ausländisches öffentliches Recht und Völkerrecht* 40: 1980 p 414-415.

1981

194. Generel orientering om den europæiske Menneskerettighedskonvention. *Nordisk Tidsskrift for international Ret* 50: 1981 p 99-105.

195. Theory and reality in international law. *American Society of international Law. Proceedings* 1981 p 140-148.

196. »Eigene Rechtsordnungen« – Skizze zu einigen systemanalytischen Betrachtungen über ein Problem der internationalen Organisation. *Europäische Gerichtsbarkeit und nationale Verfassungsgerichtsbarkeit. Festschrift für Hans Kutscher.* Baden-Baden 1981 p 415-436. (In English, see No 198).

197. Anm. af Claus Gulmann: Handelshindringer i EF-Retten. 1980. *UfR* 1981 B 285-288.

1983

198. Autonomous legal orders: Some considerations relating to a systems analysis of international organizations in the world legal order. *The international and comparative law quarterly* 32: 1983 p 559-576. (Translated from: »Eigene Rechtsordnungen«. 1981. (See No 196)).

1988

199. Les organes des organisations internationales. *Manuel sur les organisations internationales*. Nijhoff, Dordrecht 1988 p 81-178 Jurisdictions spéciales. Ibid. p 166-178. (Manuscript from 1980 revised by Ole Due and Pierre Pescatore).

B. Systematisk del
Systematic Section

1. Juriststanden. Biografi. *The legal profession. Biography:* 6,7, 9, 77, 86, 88, 144, 150, 185.
2. Forfatningsret. *Constitutional law:* 22, 31, 39, 61, 62, 66, 76, 82, 90, 92, 95, 103-105, 108, 111, 113, 116, 117, 122, 123, 138, 155, 163, 165, 167-170, 175, 178.
3. Forvaltningsret. *Administrative law:* 31, 45, 51, 54, 73, 79, 84, 94, 105, 116, 156, 192.
4. Retspleje. *Courts.* Procedure: 31, 51, 157, 173, 177.
5. Folkeret. *Public international law.*
   a. Almindeligt og blandet. *General and miscellaneous:* 1, 2, 3, 13, 16, 21, 26, 36, 37, 49, 59, 62, 65-67, 69, 82, 85, 96-99, 101, 102, 107, 115, 121, 125, 128-130, 139, 145, 151, 153, 158, 161, 167, 171, 179, 188, 190, 191, 195.
   b. Traktater. *Treaties:* 4, 5, 10-12, 14, 117, 123, 127, 133, 134, 136, 159.
   c. Havet. Stræder. *The sea. Straits:* 15, 34, 38, 83, 87, 91, 110, 119, 140, 146, 162, 182.
6. Menneskerettigheder. *Human rights:* 19, 28, 32, 41, 42, 50, 53, 57, 64, 68, 72, 75, 78, 89, 93, 100, 106, 114, 118, 120, 124, 126, 127, 132-137, 141-143, 147, 152, 154, 160, 172, 174, 180, 181, 183, 184, 186-190, 194.
7. International organisation. *International organization.*
   a. Almindeligt og blandet. *General and miscellaneous:* 18, 25, 40, 46, 71, 76, 109, 131, 156, 196, 198, 199.
   b. Forenede Nationer, FN. *United Nations, UN:* 23, 24, 35, 41, 43, 63, 74, 81, 148, 176.
   c. Europarådet. *Council of Europe:* 20, 47, 48.
8. Europæiske Fællesskaber, EF. *European Communities, EC:* 80, 90, 103, 104, 108, 111, 155, 158, 161, 164-166, 168, 169, 173, 174, 184, 186, 187, 192, 193, 197.
9. Diverse. *Miscellaneous:* 3, 8, 17, 27, 29, 30, 39, 44, 52, 56, 58, 60, 112, 119, 149, 185.